How to access your on-line resources

Kaplan Financial students will have a MyKaplan account and these extra resources will be available to you online. You do not need to register again, as this process was completed when you enrolled. If you are having problems accessing online materials, please ask your course administrator.

If you are not studying with Kaplan and did not purchase your book via a Kaplan website, to unlock your extra online resources please go to **www.en-gage.co.uk** (even if you have set up an account and registered books previously). You will then need to enter the ISBN number (on the title page and back cover) and the unique pass key number contained in the scratch panel below to gain access.

You will also be required to enter additional information during this process to set up or confirm your account details.

If you purchased through the Kaplan Publishing website you will automatically receive an e-mail invitation to register your details and gain access to your content. If you do not receive the e-mail or book content, please contact Kaplan Publishing.

Your code and information

This code can only be used once for the registration of one book online. This registration and your online content will expire when the final sittings for the examinations covered by this book have taken place. Please allow one hour from the time you submit your book details for us to process your request.

Please scratch the film to access your unique code.

Please be aware that this code is case-sensitive and you will need to include the dashes within the passcode, but not when entering the ISBN.

CIMA 2019 Professional Examinations

Management Level

Subject F2

Advanced Financial Reporting

EXAM PRACTICE KIT

British Library Cataloguing-in-Publication Data

A catalogue record for this book is available from the British Library.

Published by:

Kaplan Publishing UK
Unit 2 The Business Centre
Molly Millar's Lane
Wokingham
Berkshire
RG41 2QZ

ISBN: 978-1-83996-249-3

© Kaplan Financial Limited, 2022

The text in this material and any others made available by any Kaplan Group company does not amount to advice on a particular matter and should not be taken as such. No reliance should be placed on the content as the basis for any investment or other decision or in connection with any advice given to third parties. Please consult your appropriate professional adviser as necessary. Kaplan Publishing Limited, all other Kaplan group companies, the International Accounting Standards Board, and the IFRS Foundation expressly disclaim all liability to any person in respect of any losses or other claims, whether direct, indirect, incidental, consequential or otherwise arising in relation to the use of such materials. Printed and bound in Great Britain.

Kaplan Publishing's learning materials are designed to help students succeed in their examinations. In certain circumstances, CIMA can make post-exam adjustment to a student's mark or grade to reflect adverse circumstances which may have disadvantaged a student's ability to take an exam or demonstrate their normal level of attainment (see CIMA's Special Consideration policy). However, it should be noted that students will not be eligible for special consideration by CIMA if preparation for or performance in a CIMA exam is affected by any failure by their tuition provider to prepare them properly for the exam for any reason including, but not limited to, staff shortages, building work or a lack of facilities etc.

Similarly, CIMA will not accept applications for special consideration on any of the following grounds:

- failure by a tuition provider to cover the whole syllabus
- failure by the student to cover the whole syllabus, for instance as a result of joining a course part way through
- failure by the student to prepare adequately for the exam, or to use the correct pre-seen material
- errors in the Kaplan Official Study Text, including sample (practice) questions or any other Kaplan content or
- errors in any other study materials (from any other tuition provider or publisher).

Acknowledgements

This product contains copyright material and trademarks of the IFRS Foundation®. All rights reserved. Used under licence from the IFRS Foundation®. Reproduction and use rights are strictly limited. For more information about the IFRS Foundation and rights to use its material please visit www.ifrs.org.

Disclaimer: To the extent permitted by applicable law the Board and the IFRS Foundation expressly disclaims all liability howsoever arising from this publication or any translation thereof whether in contract, tort or otherwise (including, but not limited to, liability for any negligent act or omission) to any person in respect of any claims or losses of any nature including direct, indirect, incidental or consequential loss, punitive damages, penalties or costs.

Information contained in this publication does not constitute advice and should not be substituted for the services of an appropriately qualified professional.

IFRS

The IFRS Foundation logo, the IASB logo, the IFRS for SMEs logo, the 'Hexagon Device', 'IFRS Foundation', 'eIFRS', 'IAS', 'IASB', 'IFRS for SMEs', 'IASs', 'IFRS', 'IFRSs', 'International Accounting Standards' and 'International Financial Reporting Standards', 'IFRIC', NIIF® and 'SIC' are **Trade Marks** of the IFRS Foundation.

IFRS

Trade Marks

The Foundation has trade marks registered around the world (**'Trade Marks'**) including 'IAS®', 'IASB®', 'IFRIC®', 'IFRS®', the IFRS® logo, 'IFRS for SMEs®', IFRS for SMEs® logo, the 'Hexagon Device', 'International Financial Reporting Standards®', NIIF® and 'SIC®'.

Further details of the Foundation's Trade Marks are available from the Licensor on request.

CONTENTS

	Page
Index to questions and answers	P.7
Exam techniques	P.9
Syllabus guidance, learning objectives and verbs	P.11
Approach to revision	P.15
Syllabus grids	P.17
Tables and formulae	P.23

Section

1	Objective test questions	1
2	Answers to objective test questions	91
3	References	157

This document references IFRS® Standards and IAS® Standards, which are authored by the International Accounting Standards Board (the Board), and published in the 2020 IFRS Standards Red Book.

Quality and accuracy are of the utmost importance to us so if you spot an error in any of our products, please send an email to mykaplanreporting@kaplan.com with full details.

Our Quality Co-ordinator will work with our technical team to verify the error and take action to ensure it is corrected in future editions.

INDEX TO QUESTIONS AND ANSWERS

OBJECTIVE TEST QUESTIONS

	Page number	
	Question	Answer
Financing capital projects (Questions 1 to 30)	1	91
Long term finance	1	91
Cost of capital and yield to maturity	3	92
Financial reporting standards (Questions 31 to 94)	7	95
IAS 32 & IFRS 9 *Financial instruments*	7	95
IAS 33 *Earnings per share*	13	101
IFRS 16 *Leases*	16	102
IFRS 15 *Revenue from contracts with customers*	17	104
IAS 37 *Provisions, contingent liabilities and contingent assets*	20	107
IAS 38 *Intangible assets*	21	107
IAS 12 *Taxation*	23	109
IAS 24 *Related parties*	24	110
IAS 21 Foreign currency transactions	25	110
Group accounts (Questions 95 to 154)	27	111
Subsidiaries	27	111
Associates and joint arrangements	38	120
Consolidated statement of cash flows and CSOCIE	42	123
Foreign currency consolidations	46	125
Integrated reporting (Questions 155 to 159)	50	128
Analysing financial statements (Questions 160 to 208)	51	129
Random question tests	72	139
Test 1	72	139
Test 2	75	142
Test 3	79	146
Test 4	82	149
Test 5	86	152

EXAM TECHNIQUES

COMPUTER-BASED ASSESSMENT

Golden rules

1. Make sure you have completed the compulsory 15-minute tutorial before you start the test. This tutorial is available through the CIMA website and focusses on the functionality of the exam. You cannot speak to the invigilator once you have started.

2. These exam practice kits give you plenty of exam style questions to practise so make sure you use them to fully prepare.

3. Attempt all questions, there is no negative marking.

4. Double check your answer before you put in the final answer although you can change your response as many times as you like.

5. Not all questions will be multiple choice questions (MCQs) – you may have to fill in missing words or figures.

6. Identify the easy questions first and get some points on the board to build up your confidence.

7. Attempt 'wordy' questions first as these may be quicker than the computation style questions. This will relieve some of the time pressure you will be under during the exam.

8. If you don't know the answer, flag the question and attempt it later. In your final review before the end of the exam try a process of elimination.

9. Work out your answer on the whiteboard provided first if it is easier for you. There is also an onscreen 'scratch pad' on which you can make notes. You are not allowed to take pens, pencils, rulers, pencil cases, phones, paper or notes into the testing room.

SYLLABUS GUIDANCE, LEARNING OBJECTIVES AND VERBS

A CIMA 2019 PROFESSIONAL QUALIFICATION

Details regarding the content of the CIMA 2019 professional qualification can be located within the CIMA 2019 professional qualification syllabus document.

You can use the following diagram showing the whole structure of your qualification to help you keep track of your progress. Make sure you seek appropriate advice if you are unsure about your progression through the qualification.

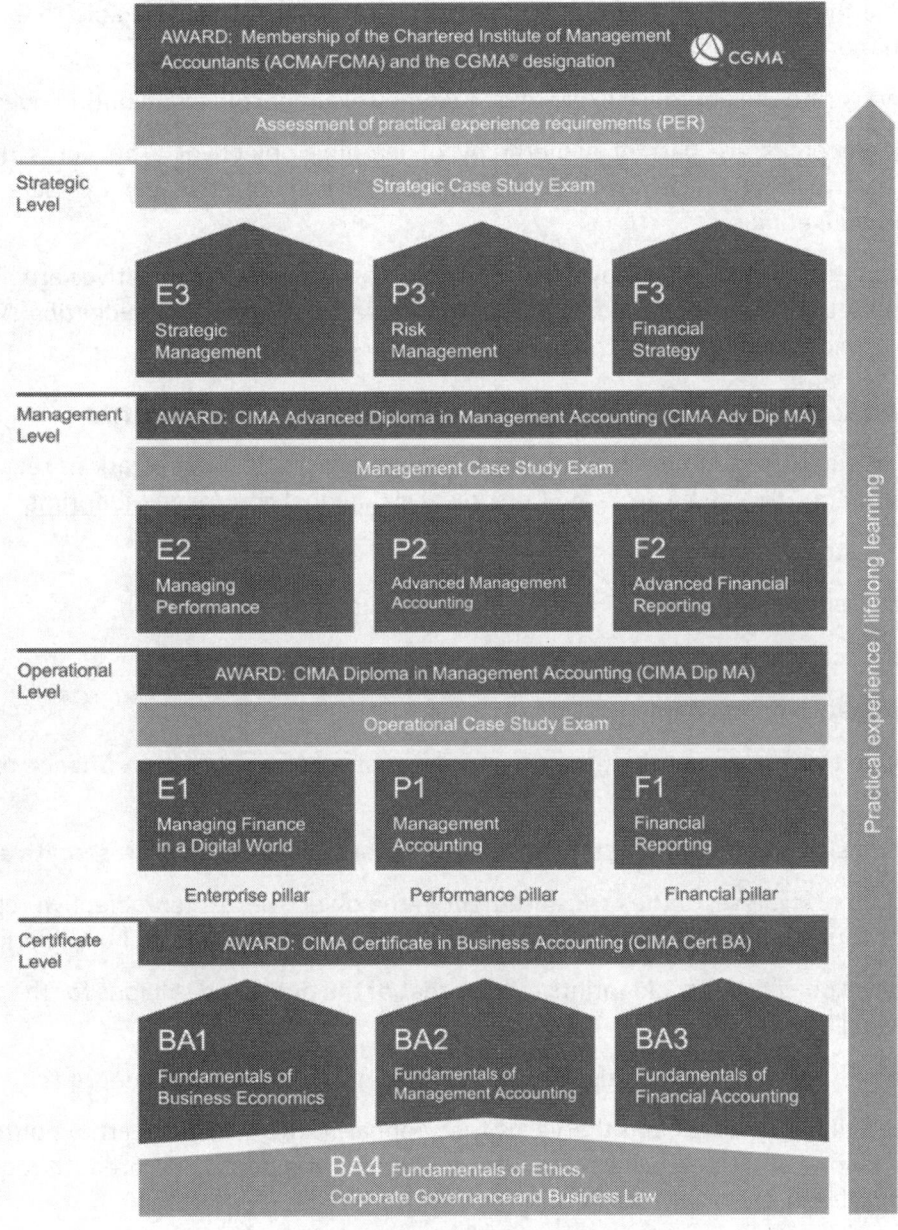

Reproduced with permission from CIMA

SUBJECT F2: ADVANCED FINANCIAL REPORTING

B STUDY WEIGHTINGS

A percentage weighting is shown against each exam content area in the exam blueprint. This is intended as a guide to the proportion of study time each topic requires.

All component learning outcomes will be tested.

The weightings do not specify the number of marks that will be allocated to topics in the examination.

C LEARNING OUTCOMES

Each subject within the qualification is divided into a number of broad syllabus topics. The topics contain one or more lead learning outcomes, related component learning outcomes and indicative knowledge content.

A learning outcome has two main purposes:

1. to define the skill or ability that a well-prepared candidate should be able to exhibit in the examination
2. to demonstrate the approach likely to be taken by examiners in examination questions.

The learning outcomes are part of a hierarchy of learning objectives. The verbs used at the beginning of each learning outcome relate to a specific learning objective, e.g. Evaluate alternative approaches to budgeting.

The verb 'evaluate' indicates a high-level learning objective. As learning objectives are hierarchical, it is expected that at this level students will have knowledge of different budgeting systems and methodologies and be able to apply them.

The examination blueprints and representative task statements

CIMA have also published examination blueprints giving learners clear expectations regarding what is expected of them. This can be accessed here www.cimaglobal.com/examblueprints

The blueprint is structured as follows:

- Exam content sections (reflecting the syllabus document)
- Lead and component outcomes (reflecting the syllabus document)
- Representative task statements.

A representative task statement is a plain English description of what a CIMA finance professional should know and be able to do.

The content and skill level determine the language and verbs used in the representative task.

CIMA will test up to the level of the task statement in the objective test (an objective test question on a particular topic could be set at a lower level than the task statement in the blueprint).

The format of the objective test blueprints follows that of the published syllabus for the 2019 CIMA Professional Qualification.

Weightings for content sections are also included in the individual subject blueprints.

A list of the learning objectives and the verbs that appear in the syllabus learning outcomes and examinations follows and these will help you to understand the depth and breadth required for a topic and the skill level the topic relates to.

CIMA verb hierarchy

Skill level	Verbs used	Definition
Level 5 Evaluation How you are expected to use your learning to evaluate, make decisions or recommendations	Advise	Counsel, inform or notify
	Assess	Evaluate or estimate the nature, ability or quality of
	Evaluate	Appraise or assess the value of
	Recommend	Propose a course of action
	Review	Assess and evaluate in order, to change if necessary
Level 4 Analysis How you are expected to analyse the detail of what you have learned	Align	Arrange in an orderly way
	Analyse	Examine in detail the structure of
	Communicate	Share or exchange information
	Compare and contrast	Show the similarities and/or differences between
	Develop	Grow and expand a concept
	Discuss	Examine in detail by argument
	Examine	Inspect thoroughly
	Interpret	Translate into intelligible or familiar terms
	Monitor	Observe and check the progress of
	Prioritise	Place in order of priority or sequence for action
	Produce	Create or bring into existence
Level 3 Application How you are expected to apply your knowledge	Apply	Put to practical use
	Calculate	Ascertain or reckon mathematically
	Conduct	Organise and carry out
	Demonstrate	Prove with certainty or exhibit by practical means
	Prepare	Make or get ready for use
	Reconcile	Make or prove consistent/compatible
Level 2 Comprehension What you are expected to understand	Describe	Communicate the key features of
	Distinguish	Highlight the differences between
	Explain	Make clear or intelligible/state the meaning or purpose of
	Identify	Recognise, establish or select after consideration
	Illustrate	Use an example to describe or explain something
Level 1 Knowledge What you are expected to know	List	Make a list of
	State	Express, fully or clearly, the details/facts of
	Define	Give the exact meaning of
	Outline	Give a summary of

SUBJECT F2: ADVANCED FINANCIAL REPORTING

Stage 2: Question practice

Follow the order of revision of topics as recommended in the revision table plan below and attempt the questions in the order suggested.

Try to avoid referring to text books and notes and the model answer until you have completed your attempt.

Try to answer the question in the allotted time.

Review your attempt with the model answer and assess how much of the answer you achieved in the allocated exam time.

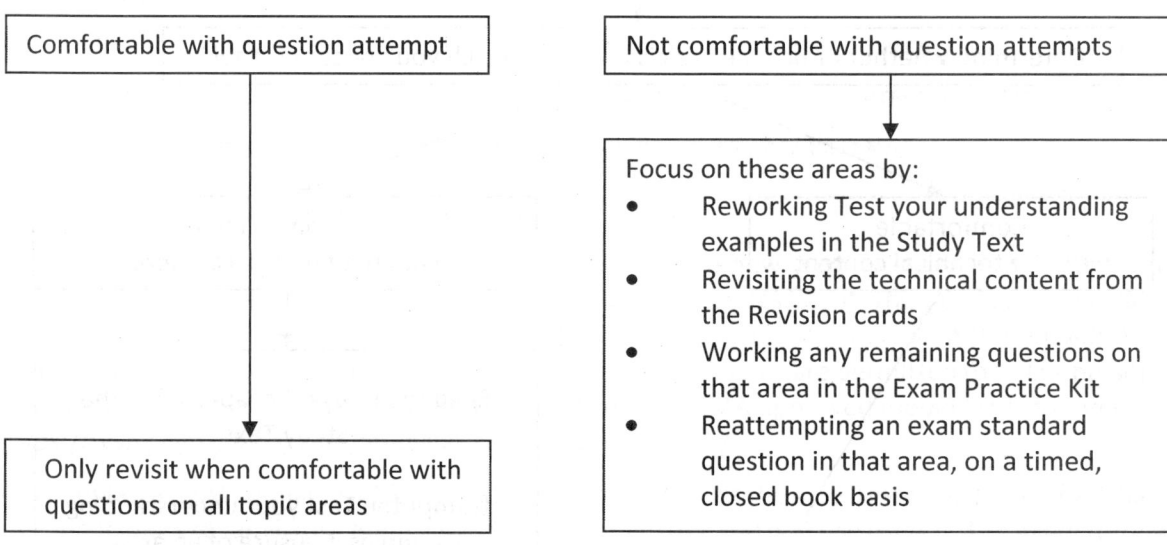

Stage 3: Final pre-exam revision

We recommend that you **attempt at least one ninety minute mock examination** containing a set of previously unseen exam standard questions.

It is important that you get a feel for the breadth of coverage of a real exam without advanced knowledge of the topic areas covered – just as you will expect to see on the real exam day.

Ideally a mock examination offered by your tuition provider should be sat in timed, closed book, real exam conditions.

SYLLABUS GRIDS

F2: Advanced Financial Reporting

Analysing and communicating insights about the performance of the organisation

Content weighting

Content area		Weighting
A	Financing capital projects	15%
B	Financial reporting standards	25%
C	Group accounts	25%
D	Integrated reporting	10%
E	Analysing financial statements	25%
		100%

SUBJECT F2: ADVANCED FINANCIAL REPORTING

F2A: Financing capital projects

For selected strategic (capital investment) projects to be implemented, funds must be sourced at the right cost and at the right time. This is a key role of the finance function and shows how it enables the organisation to create value. This section looks at the sources and types of funds and how much they cost.

Lead outcome	Component outcome	Topics to be covered	Explanatory notes
1. Compare and contrast types and sources of long-term funds.	Compare and contrast: a. Long-term debt b. Equity finance c. Markets for long-term funds	• Characteristics of different types of shares and long-term debts • Ordinary and preference shares • Bonds and other types of long-term debt • Operations of stock and bond markets • Issuance of shares and bonds • Role of advisors	What are the types of funds that can be used to finance medium to long-term projects? What are their unique and shared profiles and under what conditions are they suitable for organisations seeking long-term funds? What is the impact of these funds on the risk profile of organisations? Where can these funds be sourced? What are the criteria that organisations must fulfil to access funds from these sources?
2. Calculate cost of long-term funds.	Calculate: a. Cost of equity b. Cost of debt c. Weighted average cost of capital	• Cost of equity using dividend valuation model (with or without growth in dividends) • Post-tax cost of bank borrowing • Yield to maturity of bonds and post-tax cost of bonds • Post-tax costs of convertible bonds up to and including conversion	What is the cost of each type of funds? What is the cost of the total funds used by the organisation to fund its projects? How can the organisation minimise the cost of funds whilst ensuring the availability of adequate funds at the right time and at the same time maintaining an appropriate risk profile?

F2B: Financial reporting standards

The finance function is responsible for narrating how organisations create and preserve value. Different types of narratives are used for different audiences. Financial reporting is used for external stakeholders. This section examines the building blocks for constructing the narratives in the financial statements. It covers the key financial reporting standards on which the financial statements will be based.

Lead outcome	Component outcome	Topics to be covered	Explanatory notes
1. Explain relevant financial reporting standards for revenue, leases, financial instruments, intangible assets and provisions.	Explain the financial reporting standards for: a. Revenue b. Leases c. Provisions d. Financial instruments e. Intangible assets f. Income taxes g. Effect of changes in foreign currency rates	• IFRS 15 – Revenue from Contracts with Customers • IFRS 16 – Leases • IAS 37 – Provisions, Contingent Liabilities and Contingent Assets • IFRS 9 – Financial Instruments • IAS 32 – Financial Instruments: Presentation • IAS 38 – Intangible Assets • IAS 12 – Income Taxes • IAS 21 – Effect of Changes in on Foreign Exchange Rates	How should important elements of the financial statement be treated in the books? What principles should underpin these? How do financial reporting standards help to ensure this? Using financial reporting standards terminology this part will be looking at issues in recognition and measurement. The most important issues will be considered here.
2. Explain relevant financial reporting standards for group accounts.	a. Explain the financial reporting standards for the key areas of group accounts	• IAS 1 – Presentation of Financial Statements • IAS 27 – Separate Financial Statements • IAS 28 – Investment in Associates and Joint Ventures • IFRS 3 – Business Combinations • FRS 5 – Non-current Assets Held for Sale or Discontinued Operations • IFRS 10 – Consolidated Financial Statements • IFRS 11 – Joint Arrangements	What are the key principles that should govern the preparation of group accounts? How are they reflected in financial reporting standards? The approach should focus on the aspects of group accounts that are essential for discussions with the rest of the business. Therefore, the emphasis should be on awareness creation and basic understanding of the technical elements.

SUBJECT F2: ADVANCED FINANCIAL REPORTING

F2C: Group accounts

Organisations sometimes acquire or merge with other organisations to improve their strategic performance, position and prospects. The performance and position of combined operations are reported through group accounts. This section covers the application of the relevant financial reporting standards to prepare group accounts. The topics covered are those that are essential to conducting conversations with different parts of the business about the performance of the group and its component parts.

Lead outcome	Component outcome	Topics to be covered	Explanatory notes
1. Prepare group accounts based on IFRS.	Prepare the following based on financial reporting standards: a. Consolidated statement of financial position b. Consolidated statement of comprehensive income c. Consolidated statement of changes in equity d. Consolidated statement of cash flows	• IAS 1 – Presentation of Financial Statements • IAS 27 – Separate Financial Statements • IAS 28 – Investment in Associates and Joint Ventures • IFRS 3 – Business Combinations • IFRS 5 – Non-current Assets Held for Sale or Discontinued Operations • IFRS 10 – Consolidated Financial Statements • IFRS 11 – Joint Arrangements	This is about the preparation of basic group accounts applying the financial reporting standards learned in the previous section. Basic understanding of the technical issues is required. Thus, it should cover the rules of consolidation, goodwill, foreign subsidiaries, minority interests and associated companies. These should be placed in the context of the organisation's strategy as executed through mergers and acquisitions and the setting up of subsidiaries. In addition, it can be linked to the performance management of responsibility centres.
2. Discuss additional disclosure issues related to the group accounts.	Discuss disclosure requirements related to: a. Transaction between related parties b. Earnings per share	• IAS 24 – Related Party Disclosures • IAS 33 – Earnings Per Share	What other issues should be disclosed outside the financial statements? Why? Again, the focus is on building awareness and basic understanding of the technical issues in order to equip finance professionals to conduct meaningful discussions with the rest of the organisation about the performance, position and potential of the organisation.

F2D: Integrated reporting

In a multi-stakeholder world, there has been a call for broader forms of reporting to cover wider audiences and issues of concern to them. The International Integrated Reporting Framework developed by the International Integrated Reporting Council (IIRC) is one of the most influential frameworks that seeks to fulfil this role. This section introduces candidates to the Framework and its components.

Lead outcome	Component outcome	Topics to be covered	Explanatory notes
1. Discuss the International <IR> Framework activities.	a. Describe the role of the International Integrated Reporting Council. b. Explain integrated thinking. c. Discuss the International <IR> Framework.	• Context of integrated reporting • International Integrated Reporting Council • Integrated thinking • International <IR> Framework • Benefits and limitations of the Framework	This section looks at the International <IR> Framework as a means of addressing the need for wider forms of reporting in a multi-stakeholder world. It introduces the role of the IIRC and uses the concept of integrated thinking as the foundational concept of the International <IR> Framework. It also discusses the Framework, its benefits and limitations.
2. Explain the Six Capitals of Integrated Reporting.	Explain the measurement and disclosure issues of: a. Financial capital b. Manufactured capital c. Intellectual capital d. Human capital e. Social and relationship capital f. Natural capital	• Definition of the six capitals • Measurement and disclosure issues relating to the six capitals	The six capitals are a key part of the International <IR> Framework. This section defines the six capitals and explains the measurement and disclosure issues relating to them.

SUBJECT F2: ADVANCED FINANCIAL REPORTING

F2E: Analysing financial statements

The analyses of financial statements enable organisations to explain their performance and to compare their performance and prospects over time and against others. It can show how vulnerable they and their business models are to disruption. This section shows how these analyses are conducted and their limitations.

Lead outcome	Component outcome	Topics to be covered	Explanatory notes
1. Analyse financial statements of organisations.	Analyse financial statements to provide insight on: a. Performance b. Position c. Adaptability d. Prospects	• Ratio analysis • Interpretation of ratios • Reporting of ratios along the dimensions of the Gartner Data Analytics maturity model – descriptive, diagnostic, predictive and prescriptive • Link to organisation's business model	The financial statements narrate how organisations create and preserve value using financial numbers. Analyses of financial statements allows finance professionals to go beyond the numbers and put the narrative into everyday business language to facilitate discussions and collaboration with the rest of the organisation. The analysis could be based on the Gartner Data Analytics model which presents information as descriptive, diagnostic, predictive and prescriptive. Thus, it will cover hindsight, insight and foresight into the organisation's performance, position, resilience (or adaptability) and prospects. The analyses can be linked to the organisation's business model.
2. Recommend actions based on insights from the interpretation of financial statements.	a. Recommend actions	• Linkages between different areas of performance • Predictive and prescriptive ratios • Impact of recommendations on wider organisational ecosystem	Draw logical conclusions from the analysis. The focus is mainly predictive and prescriptive areas of data analytics. The recommendations should also be organisation wide and must encompass the ecosystem. A link with the business model framework in E2 is essential.
3. Discuss the limitations of the tools used for interpreting financial statements.	Discuss: a. Data limitations b. Limitations of ratio analysis	• Quality and type of data used • Comparability – both in segment and internationally	What are the limitations of the data and techniques used in the analyses of financial statements? How do they affect the recommendations? How could they be overcome?

TABLES AND FORMULAE

Information concerning formulae and tables will be provided via the CIMA website: www.cimaglobal.com.

Section 1

OBJECTIVE TEST QUESTIONS

FINANCING CAPITAL PROJECTS

LONG TERM FINANCE

1   Which TWO of the following statements are true?

   A   Entities must be listed on a recognised stock exchange in order to be able to raise finance from the capital markets

   B   Only equity shares can be traded in the capital markets × bonds as well. (debt instruments)

   C   Bond holders are lenders of debt finance regardless of being traded on the capital markets

   An unlisted can issue shares, but not on the stock market eg. by using a rights issues to existing shareholders.
   D   If an entity is not listed on a stock market it cannot issue new shares ×

   E   The primary function of a stock market is to enable investors to buy and sell investments
   Secondary ←   entities to raise finance

2   Complete the sentences below by placing one of the following options in each of the spaces.

   | general assets | preferable |
   | a specific asset | less preferable |

   A floating charge is when debt is secured against _general assets_ of the entity and this type of charge is considered _less preferable_ to a fixed charge from the lenders point of view.

3   Which one of the following statements is true in respect of raising equity finance?

   A   A rights issue is cheaper than a public share issue

   B   If an entity raises equity finance by way of a rights issue this would result in a flotation → the process of offering a company's shares for sale on the stock m° for 1st time

   C   A rights issue will not result in a dilution to the existing shareholders' percentage ownership in the entity × if fully subscribed.

   D   A rights issue is when equity shares are available to be purchased by ~~institutional investors only~~ all shareholders

1

SUBJECT F2: ADVANCED FINANCIAL REPORTING

4 DF has raised finance via a rights issue of 1 for 5 at $2.25 per share. The shares were quoted at $2.75 prior to the rights issue.

The **theoretical ex rights price** is:

- A $2.33
- B $2.50
- C $2.65
- **D** $2.67

$$\frac{5 \times 2.75 + 1 \times 2.25}{6} = 2.67$$

5 Complete the sentences below by placing one of the following options in each of the spaces.

cum rights (before)	ex rights

When a rights issue is announced, the existing shares will be traded _cum rights_ up to the date of the issue. After the issue takes place, the shares will then be traded _ex rights_.

6 Which one of the following statements is **NOT** a characteristic of **cumulative preference shares**?

- A   Preference dividends must be paid before ordinary dividends can be paid ✓
- B   The entity cannot claim tax relief on preference dividends paid
- C   If a dividend is not paid, it must be paid in a future period together with the normal dividend for that year ✓
- **D**   The directors can choose whether to pay the preference dividend or whether to delay it until a future period. _Directors are required to pay the preference dividend if sufficient distributable profits are available._

7 Which **TWO** of the following statements are **NOT** characteristics of **ordinary shares**?

- A   Dividends are paid at the discretion of the directors ✓
- B   Dividends are treated as a distribution of earnings and are paid out of post-tax profits
- **C**   On the winding up of the entity, the shareholders will receive a payout before other types of shareholder. _Preference 1st._
- **D**   The dividend payment will **not** be a fixed proportion of the nominal value of the shares → _determined by directors_
- E   The shareholders have voting rights

8 ZX has made a rights issue of 1 for 3 at $6.75 per share. The shares were quoted at $7.50 prior to the rights issue.

$$\frac{3 \times 7.50 + 1 \times 6.75}{4} = 7.31$$

Calculate the theoretical ex rights price. State your answer in $ to two decimal places.

9 Which one of the following statements is **NOT** an advantage of **convertible debt**?

- A   The investor benefits from having the choice of redemption method
- B   It may reduce the cash burden for the issuing entity at the redemption date
- C   It allows the entity to offer lower coupon rates than would normally be required for debt instruments
- **D**   The entity will not have to recognise a liability on the statement of financial position ✗

→ _The liability component of convertible debt must be recognised in the SFP._

OBJECTIVE TEST QUESTIONS : SECTION 1

10 Complete the sentences below by placing one of the following options in each of the spaces.

| certainty | debt | equity | less | more | uncertainty |

The providers of equity finance face __more__ risk than the providers of debt finance because there is greater __uncertainty__ over the level of their return. As a result, __equity__ providers will require a higher level of return on their investment than __debt__ providers.

COST OF CAPITAL AND YIELD TO MATURITY

11 The ordinary shares of DS are quoted at $7.50 per share [→ ex.dividend]. A dividend of $0.60 per share is about to be paid. There is no growth in dividends expected.

Calculate the cost of equity using the dividend valuation model. State your answer as a percentage to one decimal place.

$\frac{0.6}{(7.50-0.6)} = 8.7\% \, Ke$

12 ED has just paid a dividend of 10 cents per share. ED's cost of equity (ke) is 15% and dividends are expected to grow by 3% per annum.

The ex-div share price of ED is (to the nearest cent):

- A 67 cents
- B 69 cents
- C 83 cents
- D 86 cents

$15\% = \frac{0.10(1+3\%)}{x} + 3\%$

13 Complete the sentence below by placing one of the following options in the space.

| cum div market price | ex div market price | nominal value |

When calculating the cost of preference shares, the dividend is divided by the __ex div market price__ of the preference share.

14 JK plc, a listed entity, has in issue 10,000 6% coupon $100 nominal value irredeemable bonds. The current market value of each bond is $94.50.

Calculate the yield to maturity of the bonds. Give your answer as a percentage to 1 decimal place.

$\frac{6\%}{94.50} = 6.4\%$

15 The equity shares of MC are quoted at $1.86 cum div with a dividend of 10 cents per share due to be paid. → need ex div (1.86 − 0.10)

$\frac{0.10(1+3\%)}{1.76} + 3\% = 8.9\%$

Assuming that the growth rate in dividends is 3% a year, what is the cost of equity using the dividend model? Give your answer as a percentage to 1 decimal place.

16 ZX has in issue 5% convertible bonds with $100 nominal value. Each bond is either redeemable at a premium of 2% or convertible into 15 ordinary shares in five years' time. The current share price is $6 and this price is expected to grow at 4% per annum for the next five years.

Calculate the value used as the redemption amount in the internal rate of return calculation when assessing the cost of the bond.

Give your answer in $ to two decimal places.

Bond = $100 × 1.02 = $102
Shares = $6(1+4\%)^5 × 15 = $109.50

SUBJECT F2: ADVANCED FINANCIAL REPORTING

17 RS has in issue 5% irredeemable debentures currently quoted at $88 per $100 nominal value.

RS pays corporate income tax at a rate of 20%.

The post-tax cost of debt of these irredeemable debentures to one decimal place is:

A   4.0%
B   4.5%
C   4.8%
D   5.7%

$$\frac{5\% (1-20\%)}{88} = 4.5\%$$

18 Which one of the following statements is **INCORRECT** in respect of the cost of debt?

A   The cost of debt of redeemable bonds is the internal rate of return of the relevant cash flows ✓

B   When calculating the cost of debt of redeemable bonds, the relevant cash outflows are the gross annual interest payments and the redemption value of the bonds ✓ (→ net of tax)

C   When calculating the cost of convertible debt, an assumption is made that the debt holders will choose the higher of the cash and conversion option at the date of redemption ✓

D   When redeemable bonds are traded at par, the formula for irredeemable bonds can be used to calculate the cost of debt ✗

19 OLP plc, a listed entity, has in issue 30,000 7% coupon $100 nominal value irredeemable bonds. The current market value of each bond is $92.75.

Calculate the yield to maturity of the bonds. Give your answer as a percentage to 1 decimal place.

$$\frac{7\%}{92.75} = 7.5\%$$

20 The cost of equity of MB is 12.5% and the shares are currently quoted at $6.50. A dividend has recently been paid and the expected growth in dividends is 4%.

The dividend per share that was paid out (to the nearest cent) is:

A   53 cents
B   55 cents
C   57 cents
D   81 cents

$$12.5\% = \frac{x(1+4\%)}{6.50} + 4\%$$

21 WD has a cost of equity of 10%. It has just paid a dividend of $0.13 per share and its dividends are expected to grow at 5% per annum.

Calculate WD's current share price using the dividend model. Give your answer in $ to two decimal places.

$$10\% = \frac{0.13(1+5\%)}{x} + 5\% \rightarrow \$2.73$$

OBJECTIVE TEST QUESTIONS : SECTION 1

22 GG has the following debt:

| Debt: | $120 million of long dated bonds issued at par and paying a coupon rate of 6%. The debt is currently trading at $102 per $100 nominal. |

The corporate income tax rate is 30%.

$\frac{6\% \cdot (1-30\%)}{102} = 4.12\%$

Calculate the post tax cost of debt for GG. Give your answer as a percentage to one decimal place.

23 TC has in issue 100,000 $100 par value convertible bonds. The bonds are either redeemable at a premium of 15% or convertible into 10 ordinary shares in five years' time. The current share price is $10.22 and dividends are expected to grow at 2% per annum.

When calculating the cost of the bonds, what value should be included in the internal rate of return calculation per bond at the redemption date?

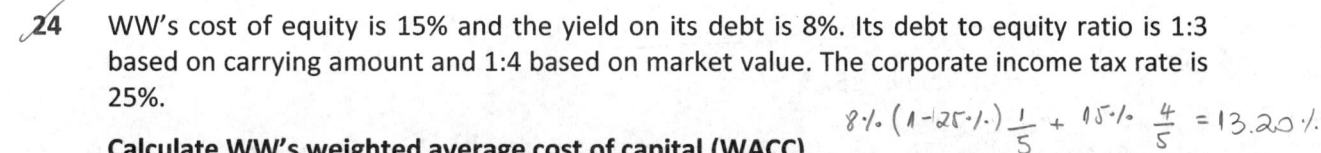

A $100.00

B $102.20

C $112.84

D $115.00

Bond = $100 \times 1.15 = \$115$ ✓

Shares = $10.22(1+2\%)^5 \times 10 = \$112.84$

24 WW's cost of equity is 15% and the yield on its debt is 8%. Its debt to equity ratio is 1:3 based on carrying amount and 1:4 based on market value. The corporate income tax rate is 25%.

Calculate WW's weighted average cost of capital (WACC).

Give your answer as a percentage to one decimal place.

$8\%(1-25\%)\frac{1}{5} + 15\% \cdot \frac{4}{5} = 13.20\%$

25 TP has the following reported in its statement of financial position as at 31 August 20X3:

Equity and liabilities	$m
Ordinary shares ($1 each)	10
Retained reserves	37
5% long dated bonds	8	→ irredeemable debt

The current share price is $1.20 and TP has consistently paid a dividend of 14 cents per share, giving a cost of equity of 11.7%. The bonds are currently trading at $87.50 per $100 nominal value. The post-tax cost of debt of the bonds is 6%.

The weighted average cost of capital (WACC) to one decimal place is:

A   8.9%

B   9.2%

C   9.4%

D   9.6%

Equity = 12m
Debt = 7m

$11.7\% \times \frac{12}{19} + 6\% \times \frac{7}{19} = 9.60\%$

5

SUBJECT F2: ADVANCED FINANCIAL REPORTING

26. PM has the following reported in its statement of financial position as at 31 March 20X2:

Equity and liabilities	$m
Ordinary shares ($1 each)	10
Retained earnings	60
7% irredeemable debentures	20

The current share price is $3.80 cum div and PM has consistently paid a dividend of 50 cents per share. The debentures are trading at $96 ex int. PM is subject to corporate income tax at a rate of 30%.

Which of the following shows the correct cost of debt and cost of equity to use in the calculation of PM's WACC?

A   Cost of debt = 4.9%
Cost of equity = 13.2%

B   Cost of debt = 5.1%
Cost of equity = 13.2%

C   Cost of debt = 4.9%
Cost of equity = 15.2%

D   Cost of debt = 5.1%
Cost of equity = 15.2%

Handwritten working:
$K_e = \dfrac{0.5}{3.8 - 0.5} = 15.2\%$
$K_d = \dfrac{7\% (1 - 30\%)}{96} = 5.1\%$

27. KC has in issue some long-dated bonds and has a post-tax cost of debt of 4.89%. The bonds are currently trading at $92 per $100 nominal.

KC pays corporate income tax at a rate of 25%.

Handwritten working: $4.89\% = \dfrac{x(1 - 25\%)}{92}$

Calculate the coupon rate of the long-dated bonds. Give your answer to the nearest whole percentage. 6%

28. JN plc has 1 million $0.50 par value shares in issue that are trading at $1.22. It has recently paid a dividend of $120,000. Dividends are expected to grow at 5% per annum.

The cost of equity of JN plc, calculated using the dividend model, is:

A   9.8%
B   10.3%
C   15.3%
D   16.5%

Handwritten working: $\dfrac{0.12(1 + 5\%)}{1.22} + 5\%$

OBJECTIVE TEST QUESTIONS : SECTION 1

29 Which one of the following statements is considered to be a limitation of using the weighted average cost of capital (WACC)?

- A Entities typically fund projects/investments from an existing pool of funds rather than specifically allocating one source of finance to each project
- B If short-term finance is used to fund long term projects, it can also be included in the WACC calculation
- C Not all debt is quoted and sometimes carrying amounts are used as approximations instead → ideally reflect market values
- D WACC can be used as discount rate in net present value and internal rate of return calculations

30 FG plc, a listed entity, has 5% coupon, $100 nominal value bonds in issue. The bonds are redeemable at a premium of 12% in 4 years' time. The current market value of the bonds is $97.

The net present value of the bond price, the annual interest and final redemption value at a discount rate of 5% is $12.91 (positive). The net present value of the same amounts at a discount rate of 10% is $4.65 (negative).

Calculate the yield to maturity of the bonds. Give your answer as a percentage to one decimal place.

$$IRR = 5\% + \frac{12.91}{(12.91+4.65)} \times (10\% - 5\%) = 8.7\%$$

FINANCIAL REPORTING STANDARDS

IAS® 32 & IFRS® 9 FINANCIAL INSTRUMENTS

31 Complete the sentences below by placing one of the following options in each of the spaces.

asset	equity	interest	favourable
debt	liability	obligation	unfavourable

A financial instrument is any contract that gives rise to a financial __asset__ of one entity and a financial liability or __equity__ instrument of another entity.

A financial liability is any liability that is a contractual __obligation__ to deliver cash or another financial asset to another entity or to exchange financial assets or liabilities under __unfavourable__ conditions.

32 ROB issued 4 million $1 5% redeemable bonds on 1 January 20X1 at par. The associated costs of issue were $100,000 which were recorded as a finance cost in the statement of profit or loss. The bonds are redeemable at $4.5 million on 31 December 20X4 and the effective interest rate associated with them has been calculated at approximately 8.5%.

The interest on the bonds is payable annually in arrears and the amount due has been paid in the year to 31 December 20X1 and charged to finance costs in the statement of profit or loss. No other accounting entries have been recorded.

No other accounting entries have been recorded.

Issue cost $100,000   4,000,000   The difference to recognised:
Int paid $200,000   − 100,000 $31,500
           300,000   3,900,000 × 8.5% = $331,500

What it was recognised by Rob

SUBJECT F2: ADVANCED FINANCIAL REPORTING

The journal entry required to correct the treatment of the bonds in the financial statements of ROB for the year ended 31 December 20X1 is:

A	Dr	Liability – bonds	$100,000
	Cr	Finance costs	$100,000
B	Dr	Finance costs	$31,500
	Cr	Liability – bonds	$31,500
C	Dr	Finance costs	$131,500
	Cr	Liability – bonds	$131,500
D	Dr	Finance costs	$140,000
	Cr	Liability – bonds	$140,000

(B marked)

33 LP issued $10 million 6% convertible bonds on 1 January 20X3 at their par value. The bonds are redeemable at par on 31 December 20X7 or can be converted at that date on the basis of two $1 equity shares for every $10 of nominal value of bonds held. The prevailing market interest rate for similar bonds without conversion rights is 8%.

The equity component recognised at initial recognition of the convertible bonds was correctly recorded at a value of $794,200.

Calculate the carrying amount of the liability component that would be reflected in LP's statement of financial position at 31 December 20X3.

Give your answer to the nearest $.

Handwritten notes:
Initial recognition
Cash 10,000,000
Equity (794,200)
9,205,800

→ effective rate

Interest	Coupon	Closing
9,205,800	736,464	(600,000)	9,342,264

34 VB acquired 40,000 shares (investment) in another entity, JK, in March 20X2 for $2.68 per share. The investment was classified as fair value through comprehensive income (FVOCI) on initial recognition. The shares were trading at $2.96 per share on 31 July 20X2. Commission of 5% of the value of the transaction is payable on all purchases and disposals of shares.

Calculate the gain that would be credited to reserves in the year ended 31 July 20X2 in respect of the above financial instrument.

Give your answer to the nearest $.

Handwritten:
Shares 107,200
Comiss. 5,360
112,560

July X2
40,000 × 2.96
= 118,400

Gain = $5,840

35 AB issued a long-term debt (liability) instrument on 1 January 20X1 raising $3,400,000. The transaction costs associated with the issue were $200,000. The debt instrument has a nominal rate of interest payable of 6% and the interest is payable annually in arrears. The effective rate of interest on the instrument is approximately 7.05%.

The liability for this instrument at 31 December 20X1 will be calculated as follows:

Liability	$ 3,400,000
Opening balance	3,200,000
Plus: finance cost	225,600
Less: interest paid	(204,000)
Closing balance	X 3,221,600

Place ONE of the following options in each of the highlighted boxes in the above table:

3,200,000	3,400,000	3,600,000
204,000	225,600	239,700

36 TR often provides short term interest free loans to its employees. Loan repayments are deducted from the employee's subsequent salary until fully repaid.

In accordance with IFRS 9® *Financial Instruments* which one of the following would be a suitable classification for the loans?

A Fair value through profit or loss financial asset
B Amortised cost financial asset
C Fair value through other comprehensive income financial asset
D Amortised cost financial liability

37 On 1 January 20X2, AB issued 400,000 5% cumulative irredeemable preference shares at their nominal value of $1.00 each. The shares have been recorded within equity and the preference dividend is payable on 31 December 20X2.

Which one of the following statements is true?

A It is correct to classify the shares as equity because they are irredeemable
B Investors in AB's preferences shares face higher risk than if they invested in non-cumulative irredeemable preference shares
C The issue will be recorded by debiting investments and crediting bank
D The dividend payable should be included in AB's finance cost as a period expense

38 BG acquired an equity investment on 30 June 20X2 for $42,000 and classified the investment as FVOCI. At 31 December 20X2, the reporting date, BG recorded a gain of $18,000 in other components of equity in respect of the change in fair value of the investment.

BG then disposed of the equity investment on 31 July 20X3 for $65,000.

In relation to the transaction above, which one of the following statements is true?

A The equity investment financial asset is incorrectly classified and should be accounted using the default position of FVPL
B The financial asset has a carrying amount of $60,000 as at the 31 December 20X3
C A gain of $23,000 is held in OCI as at 31 December 20X2
D Any gains held in reserves cannot be recycled into profit or loss upon disposal

39 JH acquired 500,000 shares in X on 1 November 20X1 for $2.80 per share and classified this investment as held for trading. JH paid 0.5% commission on the value of the transaction to its broker. X's shares were trading at $3.42 on 31 December 20X1.

JH recorded the initial measurement of the shares correctly.

The journal entry required to record the subsequent measurement of the shares at 31 December 20X1 is:

	Account reference	$
Debit	Investment in shares	310,000
Credit	Profit or loss	310,000

Place ONE of the following options in each of the boxes above:

Profit or loss	303,000
Reserves	310,000

SUBJECT F2: ADVANCED FINANCIAL REPORTING

40 GT entered into a forward contract on 31 October 20X2 to purchase 1,000 ounces of gold on 30 April 20X3 at a forward price of $1,200 per ounce. At 31 December 20X2, GT's reporting date, the forward price for purchasing gold was $1,280 per ounce.

The forward contract should appear in GT's statement of financial position at 31 December 20X2 as a:

A   Financial asset of $80,000
B   Financial asset of $1,200,000
C   Financial liability of $1,200,000
D   Financial liability of $1,280,000

41 RF has purchased 10m 5% convertible bonds for $9 million redeemable in 5 years' time at a premium of 10%.

Which one of the following statements is CORRECT in respect of the above arrangement?

A   The bond will be treated as part debt and part equity upon initial recognition
B   RF will record finance costs of $500,000 in its profit or loss account
C   The bond will be classified and measured as fair value through profit or loss
D   Cash receipts of $450,000 will be received by RF each year

42 EMS issued 5 million 6% redeemable $1 preference shares redeemable in 20X8 at their nominal value on 1 January 20X2. The issue costs associated with the share issue were $200,000.

The journal entry required to initially recognise the preference shares in the financial statements of EMS at 1 January 20X2 is:

A   Dr   Bank $4,800,000
    Cr   Equity $4,800,000

B   Dr   Bank $4,800,000
    Cr   Financial liability $4,800,000

C   Dr   Bank $4,800,000
    Dr   Profit or loss $200,000
    Cr   Equity $5,000,000

D   Dr   Bank $4,800,000
    Dr   Profit or loss $200,000
    Cr   Financial liability $5,000,000

OBJECTIVE TEST QUESTIONS : SECTION 1

43 MAT made an investment in a debt financial instrument on 1 January 20X2 at its nominal value of $2,000,000. The instrument carries a fixed coupon interest rate of 7% which is receivable annually in arrears. The instrument will be redeemed for $2,265,000 on 31 December 20X5. The business model of MAT is to intend to hold debt financial assets until maturity. Transaction costs of $100,000 were paid on acquisition.

The journal entry that initially records the instrument is:

A	Dr	Investment	$1,900,000
	Cr	Bank	$1,900,000
B	Dr	Investment	$2,000,000
	Dr	Statement of profit or loss	$100,000
	Cr	Bank	$2,100,000
C	Dr	Investment	$2,100,000
	Cr	Bank	$2,100,000
D	Dr	Investment	$1,900,000
	Dr	Statement of profit or loss	$100,000
	Cr	Bank	$2,000,000

44 BN issued $6 million 7% convertible bonds on 1 January 20X1 at par. The bonds are redeemable at par on 31 December 20X4 or convertible at that date on the basis of two $1 ordinary shares for every nominal $10 of bonds. At the date of issue, the prevailing market rate of interest for similar debt without conversion rights was 9%.

The amount that should be credited to equity upon the initial recognition of the convertible bonds on 1 January 20X1 is:

A $2,400

B $391,200

C $4,320,000

D $4,639,200

45 BCL entered into a forward contract on 31 July 20X0 to purchase B$2 million at a contracted rate of A$1: B$0.64 on 31 October 20X0. The contract cost was A$nil. BCL prepares its financial statements to 31 August 20X0. At 31 August 20X0, an equivalent contract for the purchase of B$2 million could be acquired at a rate of A$1: B$0.70

The journal entry that records this instrument in the financial statements for the year ended 31 August 20X0 is:

A	Dr	Derivative asset	A$ 120,000
	Cr	Profit or loss	A$ 120,000
B	Dr	Profit or loss	A$ 120,000
	Cr	Derivative liability	A$ 120,000
C	Dr	Derivative asset	A$ 267,857
	Cr	Profit or loss	A$ 267,857
D	Dr	Profit or loss	A$ 267,857
	Cr	Derivative liability	A$ 267,857

SUBJECT F2: ADVANCED FINANCIAL REPORTING

46 EMR made an investment in a debt instrument on 1 July 20X0 at its nominal value of $4,000,000. The instrument carries a fixed coupon interest rate of 7%, which is receivable annually in arrears. The instrument will be redeemed for $4,530,000 on 30 June 20X4. Transaction costs associated with the investment were $200,000 and were paid on 1 July 20X0. The effective interest rate applicable to this instrument has been calculated at approximately 8.4%. EMR's business model is to hold debt financial assets until maturity.

The impact of the investment in the statement of profit or loss and other comprehensive income for the year ended 30 June 20X1 is:

Statement of profit or loss extract	$
Profit from operations	X
Finance income	352,800
Finance costs	BLANK
Profit before tax	X

Place ONE of the following options in each of the highlighted boxes in the above table. Place 'BLANK' against the heading not required:

227,200	280,000
319,200	336,000
352,800	444,000
BLANK	

47 JK acquired 100% of the ordinary shares of OVS on 1 July 20X1 for $2,400,000. All of JK's investment transactions are conducted by a broker who charges 2% commission on the transaction value. JK has correctly classified and recorded its investment in OVS as a FVOCI asset. At 30 June 20X2, the investment in OVS has a fair value of $2,570,000.

The journal entry required in JK's individual financial statements to record the subsequent measurement of the investment at 30 June 20X2 is:

	Account reference	$
Debit	Investment in shares	122,000
Credit	Reserves	

Place ONE of the following options in each of the boxes above:

Profit or loss	122,000
Reserves	170,000

12

OBJECTIVE TEST QUESTIONS : SECTION 1

48 CLW issued a $4 million 7% convertible bond on 1 January 20X2 at par value. The bond is redeemable at par on 31 December 20X6 or can be converted at that date on the basis of two $1 ordinary shares for every $10 of bonds held. The prevailing market interest rate for a similar bond without conversion rights was 9% per annum.

n = 5

The journal entry required to initially record the convertible bond on 1 January 20X2 is:

	Account reference	$
Debit	Bank	4,000,000
Credit	Financial Liability	3,689,200
Credit	Equity	310,800

Place ONE of the following options in each of the boxes above:

Bank	310,800
Financial asset	3,689,200
Financial liability	4,000,000
BLANK	

IAS® 33 EARNINGS PER SHARE

49 On 1 July 20X0, BNM, a listed entity, had 5 million $1 ordinary shares in issue. On 1 September 20X0, BNM made a 1 for 2 bonus issue from retained earnings. BNM generated profit after tax of $3.8 million for the year ended 30 June 20X1.

Calculate the basic earnings per share for the year ended 30 June 20X1.

Give your answer in cents to one decimal place. $0.51 ≈ 51.7

BF = 7.5/5 =

WAV = 5 × 2/12 × 1.5 + 7.5 × 10/12 = 7.50

50 On 1 October 20X1, VB, a listed entity, had 8 million $1 ordinary shares in issue. On 1 May 20X2, VB issued a further 2.4 million new $1 ordinary shares for $9.20, the full market price.

The consolidated profit for the year was $6,582,000 of which $420,000 was attributable to the non-controlling interest.

The consolidated basic earnings per share of VB for the year ended 30 September 20X2 is:

A 67.0 cents per share
B 68.5 cents per share
C 73.1 cents per share
D 77.8 cents per share

$$\frac{6,582 - 420}{8,000 \times 7/12 + (8,000 + 2,400) \times 5/12} =$$

51 CB, a listed entity, had 3,000,000 ordinary shares in issue on 1 February 20X4. On 1 March 20X4, CB made a rights issue of 1 for 4 at $6.50 per share. The issue was fully taken up by the shareholders.

CB's share price immediately prior to the rights issue was $7.50, rising to $8.25 after the issue. The theoretical ex rights price relating to the rights issue is $7.30.

→ cum right price

Calculate the weighted average number of shares that would be used in the basic earnings per share calculation for the year ended 31 January 20X5.

Give your answer to the nearest whole number of shares.

BF = 7.50/7.30 = 1.03   WAV = 3,000,000 × 1/12 × 1.03 + 3,750,000 × 11/12 = 3,694,349

52 The weighted average number of ordinary shares in issue for the year to 31 December 20X1 is 7 million and the profit for the year was $3.5 million resulting in basic earnings per share for the year of 50 cents.

Options to purchase 1,000,000 $1 ordinary shares at $3.10 per share were issued on 1 January 20X1. These options are exercisable between 1 January 20X2 and 31 December 20X4. The average market value of each $1 ordinary share during the year ended 31 December 20X1 is $4.00.

The diluted earnings per share, in cents to one decimal place, for the year ended 31 December 20X1 is:

A   34.7 cents per share
B   43.8 cents per share
C   48.0 cents per share
D   48.4 cents per share

53 FS, a listed entity, has reported a basic earnings per share of 6 cents for the year ended 31 December 20X8. FS had 10,000,000 ordinary shares in issue on 1 January 20X8. On 1 April 20X8, FS issued 2,000,000 further ordinary shares at full market price. Then, on 31 October 20X8, it made a 1 for 4 bonus issue.

Calculate the profit after tax attributable to the equity shareholders of FS for the year ended 31 December 20X8.

54 SW's basic earnings per share for the year is 30 cents, based on earnings of $3 million and a weighted average number of ordinary shares of 10 million. SW is subject to corporate income tax at a rate of 25%.

SW has a convertible instrument that has been in issue throughout the entire financial year. The liability component at the start of the year was $5 million and is being measured at amortised cost using the effective interest rate of 6%. Conversion of the instrument would result in an additional 1.2 million ordinary shares being issued.

Calculate the diluted earnings per share of SW for the year.

State your answer in cents to one decimal place.

55 When calculating the earnings figure for inclusion in the basic earnings per share calculation in accordance with IAS 33 *Earnings per Share*, which TWO of the following should be deducted from the profit after tax figure?

A   Irredeemable preference dividend payable for the current year
B   Irredeemable preference dividend that relates to a previous year but has been paid out in the current year
C   Ordinary dividend declared for the current year
D   Profit after tax attributable to the non-controlling interest
E   Redeemable preference dividend payable for the current year

OBJECTIVE TEST QUESTIONS : SECTION 1

56 SP, a listed entity, had 20,000,000 ordinary shares in issue on 1 January 20X2. On 1 June 20X2, SP made a 1 for 4 rights issue at $1.50 per share. The issue was fully taken up by the shareholders.

SP's share price immediately prior to the rights issue was $2.20 and the theoretical ex rights price relating to the rights issue is $2.06.

The basic earnings per share reported in the financial statements of SP for the year ended 31 December 20X1 was 46.2 cents.

The comparative basic earnings per share that would be presented in the financial statements of SP for the year ended 31 December 20X2 is:

A   37.0 cents per share

B   43.3 cents per share

C   46.2 cents per share

D   49.3 cents per share

57 JKL, a listed entity, had 6 million $1 ordinary shares in issue on 1 January 20X3. On 28 February 20X3, JKL made a bonus issue of 1 new ordinary share for 4 held. On 1 July JKL then issued a further 1,500,000 new $1 ordinary shares at full market price. Reported basic earnings per share for the year ended 31 December 20X2 was 98.2 cents per share.

In the financial statements of JKL for the year to 31 December 20X3, what will be the comparative figure for basic earnings per share?

Give your answer in cents to one decimal place.

58 Options to purchase 1,500,000 $1 ordinary shares at $3.50 per share were issued on 1 January 20X2. These options are exercisable between 1 January 20X5 and 31 December 20X6. The average market value of each $1 ordinary share during the year ended 31 December 20X2 is $4.75.

The 'free' shares that should be added to the weighted average number of shares in the calculation of diluted earnings per share for the year ended 31 December 20X2 is:

A   315,789

B   394,737

C   428,571

D   535,714

SUBJECT F2: ADVANCED FINANCIAL REPORTING

IFRS® 16 LEASES

59 Complete the sentence below by placing one of the following options in each of the spaces.

rental	right-of-use asset	derecognised	net investment in the lease	receivable
lease liability	the statement of profit or loss	the statement of financial position	finance	operating

For a lessor, an asset leased on an <u>OPERATING</u> lease would be held within the statement of financial position, and <u>RENT</u> income is subsequently recognised within <u>SPL</u>.

60 Hudson entered into an operating lease with a customer on 1 July 20X7 with the following terms:

- three-year non-cancellable lease of a machine
- 6 months rent free period from commencement → don't consider recording linear
- rent of $18,000 per annum payable at $1,500 a month from month 7 onwards

What is the amount that should be recorded as rental income in Hudson's statement of profit or loss for the year to 31 December 20X7?

A $0

B $7,500

C $9,000

D $18,000

18,000 × 3 =

61 FL leases a machine to JS that would have a useful life of 8 years if bought outright.

Which THREE of the following independent characteristics would be likely to indicate that FL would treat the lease as a finance lease?

A   The primary lease term is for four years and JS has the option to extend the term for a further four years for a small notional charge each year

B   FL is responsible for maintaining and repairing the machine in the event of a breakdown → should be JS, because the risk is transferred.

C   The machine is specialised in nature and has been built according to the specifications agreed by JS

D   At the end of the lease term, JS can purchase the asset at its then market value — lower than

E   If JS cancels the lease before the end of the term it will be responsible for compensating FL for lost future rentals and interest

OBJECTIVE TEST QUESTIONS : SECTION 1

62 Z entered into a finance lease agreement with a customer on 1 November 20X2. The lease was for five years, the present value of minimum lease payments was $30,000 and the interest rate implicit in the lease was 7%. The annual payment was $7,317 in arrears.

What is the amount to be shown as a non-current receivable at 31 October 20X3?

- A $18,141
- B $19,201
- C $24,271
- D $24,783

63 Screenslaver Co leases an item of property to a customer on 1 December 20X9. The lease term is 5 years. The asset has a carrying amount at the start of the lease term of $21,000. The present value of minimum lease payments is $24,000. The fair value of the asset is $25,000. The rate implicit in the lease is 3.71%. The estimated remaining economic lifetime of the asset is 7 years.

On the 1 December 20X9, which of the following balances will require a journal entry? Select all that apply.

- A Property, plant and equipment
- B Rental receipts in profit or loss
- C Right of use asset
- D Gain or loss on disposal
- E Lease receivable
- F Interest income

IFRS® 15 REVENUE FROM CONTRACTS WITH CUSTOMERS

64 Which of the following statements are true in relation to the recognition of revenue in accordance with IFRS 15 *Revenue from contracts with customers*? Select all that apply:

- A A contract must exist between the seller and the buyer
- B Performance obligations must be fully satisfied
- C Variable consideration must be included in the value of the performance obligations provided
- D The goods have been delivered to the buyer
- E The entity must identify and separate the distinct performance obligations within a contract

SUBJECT F2: ADVANCED FINANCIAL REPORTING

65 Which one of the following statements is true?

A Variable consideration is always included in the price of a sales contract *just when is highly Prob.*

B Revenue is recorded only at the point that cash is received from a customer ✗

C If a sale includes a significant financing element, revenue is limited to the present value discounted at the seller's rate of borrowing

D Non-cash consideration included in a sale is recorded at the cost of the goods sold ✗ *price at FV*

66 ST enters into a contract to develop bespoke software for a customer. Having completed development and delivered the software to the customer on 30 June 20X3, ST has invoiced the customer the agreed fixed fee of $575,000, comprising $500,000 for the development of the software and $75,000 for service and support of the software over the 3-year support period.

The revenue that should be recognised in ST's statement of profit or loss for the year ended 31 December 20X3 in respect of the above customer contract is:

A $500,000

B $512,500

C $525,000

D $575,000

67 BangersRUs (BRS) sells used cars and offers 3 years 0% finance. BRS sold a car at $6,000. The cash price of the car is $5,000. The rate of interest on the retailer's borrowing is 7%.

How much is recorded as revenue by BRS at the date of the sale?

A $4,080

B $4,896 $PV = 4,898$

C $5,000

D $6,000

68 Half-a-job Bob is an online business that helps to match the users of its website to professional tradespersons and craft workers. Users of the website require building, maintenance and repair work for their home and Half-a-job Bob provide the details of tradespersons within the local vicinity. Tradespersons will provide quotes to the users with a view to carry out the work. Once the job is agreed, Half-a-job Bob have no further involvement in the work and are not liable for the progress or outcome of the work performed. Half-a-job Bob charge a commission of 10% of any fees earned by its recommended professionals. Half-a-job Bob does not employ any full time trade workers.

During the year, Half-a-job Bob's records show that $10m of revenue was earned by its registered tradespersons through the website. 90% of recoverable fees had been received by the year end.   *not important full amount accrued.*

The revenue recorded in the statement of profit or loss of Half-a-job Bob will be:

A $0.9m

B $1m $10m \times 10\% \times 90\%$

C $9m   *Agents can only recognise revenue up to*

D $10m   *the amount of commission they earn.*

OBJECTIVE TEST QUESTIONS : SECTION 1

69 XZ sells goods to WY with a right to return. The terms of the arrangement are that the goods can be returned within 28 days of sale. Payment is not due until the returns period has elapsed. WY has full control of the goods on delivery. The total value of sales made to WY still within the 28 day returns period at 31 December 20X2, XZ's reporting date, is $1,250,000. XZ have sold to WY for a number of years and reliably estimates that 10% of these sales will be returned by WY. XZ has made a margin of 25% on the sales.

Which one of the following statements is true in respect of the above?

A Revenue recognised by XZ should be discounted to present value as the sale includes a significant financing component

B No revenue should be recognised by XZ on any of the sale items until the 28-day right of return period has elapsed

C A refund liability of $125,000 is recorded in the statement of profit or loss

D Inventory is recorded by XZ until payment is received

70 BL commenced a fixed price contract on 1 March 20X1 to construct a building on land controlled by their customer. The contract is scheduled to run for three years and the total contract price is $40 million.

The details of the contract at the reporting dates of 31 December 20X1 and 20X2 are:

Year ended 31 December:	20X1	20X2
	$m	$m
Costs incurred to date	7	18
Expected costs to complete	26	16
Cumulative work certified as complete	8	22

BL uses output methods based on work certified as complete to calculate the stage of completion.

Calculate the profit that BL would recognise on the above contract in the year ended 31 December 20X2. State your answer in $m to one decimal place.

71 Which of the following is not one of the 5 steps associated with recognising revenue as identified by IFRS 15 *Revenue from contracts with customers*?

A Allocate the transaction price to the performance obligations

B Identify the performance obligations

C Determine the transaction price

D Recognise revenue as control is transferred

E Identify the contract

SUBJECT F2: ADVANCED FINANCIAL REPORTING

72 DB commenced a contract to construct a specialised asset on 1 January 20X5 and the details at its reporting date of 31 December 20X5 are as follows:

	$000
Total contract price	3,000
Costs incurred to date:	
Attributable to work completed	1,500
Inventory purchased, not yet used	150
Expected costs to complete	350

DB uses input methods to assess progress of the contract, specifically the percentage of costs incurred to total expected costs, to calculate the stage of completion of construction contracts. DB has the legal right for repayment for work performed to date.

The profit that should be recognised in DB's statement of profit or loss for the year ended 31 December 20X5, to the nearest $000, is:

- A $300,000
- B $750,000 *(circled)*
- C $811,000
- D $825,000

Handwritten: 3,000 − 2,000; input = 1500/2000 × 1,000

73 NM commenced a two-year contract to construct an office building on 1 April 20X4. The contract had a fixed price of $26 million. NM incurred costs to 31 March 20X5, its reporting date, of $17 million and has now estimated that a further $11 million will need to be incurred to complete the contract. The work certified as complete at 31 March 20X5 is $14 million.

NM uses work certified as a percentage of contract price to calculate the progress to completion of the contract.

Handwritten: 14/26 = 53.9%

Which one of the following shows the revenue and cost of sales figures in respect of the above contract in NM's financial statements for the year ended 31 March 20X5?

- A Revenue of $14 million and cost of sales of $16 million
- B Revenue of $14 million and cost of sales of $15 million
- C Revenue of $15 million and cost of sales of $17 million
- D Revenue of $15 million and cost of sales of $15 million

Handwritten: 26, (17), (11), (2) — expected loss! PL should show the loss immediately. Revenue 14 Cost (16) balance loss (2)

IAS® 37 PROVISIONS, CONTINGENT LIABILITIES AND CONTINGENT ASSETS

74 Which one of the following costs would **not** be recognised in accordance with IAS 37 Provisions, contingent liabilities and contingent assets?

- A Expected costs of warranty repairs for goods sold under warranty prior to the reporting date ✓
- B Costs relating to closure of a division that has been announced prior to the reporting date ✓
- C Expected losses over the next 12 months from a subsidiary acquired a week before the reporting date *(handwritten: ARE PROHIBITED, NO PROVISION BECAUSE THERE IS NOT OBLIGATION)*
- D Remaining lease payments after vacating premises that cannot be sublet ✓

OBJECTIVE TEST QUESTIONS : SECTION 1

75 ES operates in the oil and gas industry and publishes an environmental and social report to demonstrate its corporate social responsibility. It is partly responsible for a recent oil leak causing damage to the local environment and is planning to voluntarily contribute to the costs of the clean-up, although it is under no legal obligation to do so. It anticipates the cost to be $500,000 but this is not certain.

Which one of the following statements is true in respect of this scenario?

A   Under no circumstances should a provision be made in the financial statements of ES as there is no legal obligation to incur the expenditure

B   There is a probable outflow of economic benefit but the timing and amount is uncertain and so a contingent liability should be included in ES's financial statements

C   A provision should be made for the clean-up costs because ES are planning to incur the expenditure and this will result in an outflow of economic benefits

D   A provision should be made for the clean-up costs if ES has created a valid expectation that it will incur the expenditure in its publication of the environmental and social report

76 IAS 37 *Provisions, contingent liabilities and contingent assets* sets criteria that must be satisfied before a provision is made or a contingent item disclosed. The accounting treatment can be summarised as follows:

Degree of probability of an outflow/inflow of resources	Liability	Asset
Virtually certain	Recognise	Recognise
Probable	Make a provision	Disclose
Possible	Disclose	Ignore
Remote	Disclose	Ignore

Place ONE of the following options in each of the shaded boxes above:

Disclose (in note)	Ignore
Make provision	Recognise

Note that each option may be used more than once.

IAS® 38 INTANGIBLE ASSETS

77 IAS 38 *Intangible Assets* sets out six criteria that must be met before development costs can be recognised.

Which THREE of the following are included in the criteria?

A   Revenues can be generated

B   Adequate cash to complete

C   The project must be technically feasible

D   Costs can be measured

E   An ability to use or sell the developed item

F   The developed item will generate a probable future economic benefit

SUBJECT F2: ADVANCED FINANCIAL REPORTING

78 Which of the following CANNOT be recognised as an intangible non-current asset in GHK's statement of financial position at 30 September 20X1?

    A   GHK spent $12,000 researching a new type of product. The research is expected to lead to a new product line in 3 years' time.

    B   GHK purchased another entity, BN on 1 October 20X0. Goodwill arising on the acquisition was $15,000.

    C   GHK purchased a brand name from a competitor on 1 November 20X0, for $65,000.

    D   GHK spent $21,000 during the year on the development of a new product. The product is being launched on the market on 1 December 20X1 and is expected to be profitable.

79 Which of the following would be capitalised as an intangible asset according to IAS 38 *Intangible Assets*?

    A $120,000 spent on testing a hydro-propulsion system for trains. The project needs further work as the propulsion system is currently not effective.

    B   A payment of $50,000 to a local university's engineering faculty to research new environmentally friendly digital engineering techniques.

    C $35,000 spent on consumer testing a new voice-controlled electric bicycle. The project is near completion and looks likely to be launched in the next twelve months. The entity is inexperienced within the market sector and, as a result, the project is expected to make an initial loss.

    D $65,000 spent on developing new packaging for energy efficient smart light bulbs. The packaging is expected to be used for many years and is expected to reduce the entity's distribution costs by $35,000 a year

80 Sybil has acquired a subsidiary, Basil, in the current year.

Basil has a brand which has been reliably valued by Sybil at $500,000, and a customer list which Sybil has been unable to value.

Which of these describes how Sybil should treat the intangible assets of Basil in their consolidated financial statements?

    A   Both the brand and the customer list should be included within goodwill.

    B   The brand should be capitalised as a separate intangible asset, whereas the customer list should be included within goodwill.

    C   Both the brand and the customer list should be capitalised as separate intangible assets.

    D   The customer list should be capitalised as a separate intangible asset, whereas the brand should be included within goodwill.

OBJECTIVE TEST QUESTIONS : SECTION 1

81 Which of the following statements relating to intangible assets is true?

- A All intangible assets must be carried at amortised cost or at an impaired amount, they cannot be revalued upwards.
- B The development of a new process which is not expected to increase sales revenues may still be recognised as an intangible asset.
- C Internally generated intellectual property developed through staff skill, know-how and expertise is capitalised as an intangible asset
- D Goodwill must be amortised over its economic lifetime.

IAS® 12 TAXATION

82 Which TWO of the following would result in a deferred tax asset?

- A A provision for warranty costs, that are tax deductible when incurred
- B Development costs capitalised in the statement of financial position, for which a tax deduction has already been claimed
- C Losses to be carried forward and offset against future expected profits
- D Property, plant and equipment with a carrying amount greater than the tax base
- E Revaluation surplus on land and buildings

83 At 1 January 20X3, SD had a deferred tax liability brought forward of $25,000 resulting from temporary differences on property, plant and equipment. At 31 December 20X3, the carrying amount of property, plant and equipment in SD's statement of financial position was $470,000 and its tax base was $365,000. The corporate income tax rate was 20%.

The impact of deferred tax in the statement of profit or loss for the year ended 31 December 20X3 is:

- A $4,000 charge
- B $4,000 credit
- C $21,000 charge
- D $21,000 credit

84 HT has an item of property, plant and equipment with a carrying amount of $400,000 and a tax base of $370,000 at 31 December 20X5. The corporate income tax rate is 20%. The deferred tax liability brought forward in respect of this property, plant and equipment is $4,000.

HT then implements a revaluation policy for the first time and revalues the property, plant and equipment to $750,000.

SUBJECT F2: ADVANCED FINANCIAL REPORTING

Which THREE of the following statements are true in respect of HT's deferred tax on the above property, plant and equipment?

A An additional temporary difference of $70,000 is created by the revaluation

B The balance on the revaluation surplus will be $280,000

C The deferred tax liability after the revaluation is $76,000

D The overall charge to profit or loss in respect of deferred tax on the property, plant and equipment in the year will be $2,000

E The overall charge to profit or loss in respect of deferred tax on the property, plant and equipment in the year will be $72,000

F The revaluation has no impact on deferred tax as it does not affect the tax base

85 QW prepares its financial statements to 31 December each year. On 1 January 20X1, QW made losses of $1m which can be rolled forward for tax purposes.

When recognising deferred tax for the year ended 31 December 20X1, QW should:

A recognise a deferred tax liability resulting from the losses

B ignore the losses as there is no asset or liability recognised in the statement of financial position and therefore no temporary difference

C record any deferred tax implications of the losses against reserves to match against the accounting treatment of the transaction causing the deferred tax

D recognise a deferred tax asset that equates to the losses expected to be offset against future profits multiplied by the tax rate

86 Complete the sentences below by placing one of the following options in each of the spaces.

| deductible | asset |
| taxable | liability |

If the carrying amount of an asset exceeds its tax base, then there is a _taxable_ temporary difference and this will result in a deferred tax _liability_.

IAS® 24 RELATED PARTIES

87 Which THREE of the following would be considered related parties of CV, in accordance with IAS 24 *Related Party Disclosures*?

A A shareholder who owns 25% of the ordinary shares of CV and exerts significant influence

B A subsidiary of CV, with whom CV does not trade

C CV's biggest customer, providing 60% of CV's annual revenue

D CV's main supplier of finance, providing significant loans to the business

E The employees of CV

F The spouse of CV's managing director

OBJECTIVE TEST QUESTIONS : SECTION 1

88 AB owns 80% of CD. CD owns 40% of EF, over which it exercises significant influence. AB also shares joint control of JV, a separate entity, with PQ via a joint arrangement.

Which one of the following sets would be considered related parties of AB, in accordance with international financial reporting standards?

A   CD, EF and PQ

B   CD, EF and JV

C   CD, JV and PQ

D   CD, EF, JV and PQ

IAS 21 FOREIGN CURRENCY TRANSACTIONS

89 An entity based in the US sells goods to the UK for £400,000 on 2 February 20X3 when the exchange rate was $1/£0.65.

The balance remains outstanding as at the year-end, 28 February 20X3, when the rate of exchange is $/£0.60.

How does the entity account for the sale at 2 February 20X3?

A   Dr Receivables $240,000   Cr Revenue $240,000

B   Dr Cash $666,667   Cr Revenue $666,667

C   Dr Revenue $260,000   Cr Receivables $260,000

D   Dr Receivables $615,385   Cr Revenue $615,385

90 Trumpt Towers (TT), whose functional currency is the US$, sells goods to a customer in Europe for €600,000 on 31 December 20X5 when the exchange rate was $1/€0.85.

The customer pays in February 20X6 when the rate was $/€0.80.

Complete the sentence below by placing one of the following options into each of the spaces.

On receipt of the payment from the customer, TT will record a foreign currency _____ of $_____ which will be recorded within _____.

$30,000	Gain
$44,118	Loss
$480,000	Profit or loss
$750,000	Other comprehensive income

91 Complete the sentence below by placing one of the following options into each of the spaces.

IAS 21 *The Effects of Changes in Foreign Exchange Rates* states unsettled _____ items, e.g. receivables, must be _____ at the reporting date and _____ items are _____.

| monetary |
| non-monetary |
| retranslated using the closing rate |
| left at historical rate |

25

SUBJECT F2: ADVANCED FINANCIAL REPORTING

92 IAS 21 *The Effects of Changes in Foreign Exchange Rates* defines the term 'functional currency'.

Which of the following is the correct definition of 'functional currency'?

- A The currency in which the financial statements are presented
- B The currency of the country where the reporting entity is located
- C The currency that mainly influences sales prices and operating costs
- D The currency of the primary economic environment in which an entity operates

93 Sunshine is an entity with a reporting date of 31 December 20X1 and a functional currency of dollars ($). On 30 June 20X1, it purchased land from overseas on credit at a cost of 30 million dinars. The payment is due in 12 months' time. The land is an item of property, plant and equipment and is measured using the cost model.

Exchange rates are as follows:

	Dinars: $1
As at 30 June 20X1	3.0
As at 31 December 20X1	2.0
Average rate for year-ended 31 December 20X1	2.5

The fair value of the land at 31 December 20X1 was 32 million dinars.

Which of the following journals is required to be posted as at 31 December 20X1?

- A Dr PPE $10m Cr Payables $10m
- B Dr PPE $2m Cr OCI $2m
- C Dr Profit or loss $5m Cr Payables $5m
- D Dr Payables $2m Cr Profit or loss $2m

94 JPS is an entity with a reporting date of 31 December 20X1 and a functional currency of dollars ($). On 30 June 20X1, it purchased land from overseas on credit at a cost of 15 million dinars. The land is measured using the cost model.

Exchange rates are as follows:

	Dinars: $1
As at 30 June 20X1	3.0
As at 31 December 20X1	2.0

What is the carrying amount of the land as at 31 December 20X1?

- A $5 million
- B $7.5 million
- C $30 million
- D $45 million

GROUP ACCOUNTS

SUBSIDIARIES

95 LP is considering selling one of its wholly owned subsidiaries, GH, after the current year end, however, it is concerned that it will struggle to find a buyer due to GH's poor profitability. LP uses GH as a supplier and has decided to increase its purchase prices in the final three months of the accounting period in order to boost GH's profits. As LP already trades with GH it does not believe that any additional disclosures need to be made to reflect this revised pricing.

It intends to recover the increase in cost by arranging a significant dividend payment prior to the disposal but after the year end.

In respect of this arrangement, which one of the following statements is true?

- A Any intra-group transactions are eliminated in the consolidated financial statements and, therefore, this does not create an ethical issue
- B As the cost will be recovered via the dividend payment there is no ethical issue
- C It is a deliberate attempt to mislead potential acquirers who might rely on GH's financial statements and as a result the directors are acting unethically
- D The proposed accounting treatment is in accordance with international financial reporting standards and therefore there is no ethical issue

96 Which one of the following statements is INCORRECT in respect of the recognition of goodwill in consolidated financial statements?

- A If goodwill at acquisition is negative, it should be credited to profit or loss immediately
- B Changes in the fair value of the subsidiary's net assets arising after acquisition are dealt with as post-acquisition adjustments in line with group accounting policies
- C Contingent consideration should only be recognised in the goodwill calculation if it is considered probable that it will be paid
- D The various elements of consideration paid should be measured at their fair value at the date of acquisition

97 RF acquired 80% of the ordinary shares of YT on 1 January 20X1. The carrying amount of YT's net assets at 1 January 20X1 was $850,000. The fair value of the net assets of YT was considered to be the same as their carrying amount with the following exceptions:

- The fair value of property, plant and equipment was $650,000 higher than carrying amount.
- The fair value of inventories was considered to be $25,000 higher than carrying amount.
- YT had disclosed a contingent liability in the notes to its financial statements. Its fair value was considered to be $100,000 at acquisition and, at 31 December 20X1, was $110,000.

RF is preparing the consolidated financial statements for the year ended 31 December 20X1.

SUBJECT F2: ADVANCED FINANCIAL REPORTING

The fair value of net assets that would be reflected in the calculation of goodwill arising on the acquisition of YT in RF's consolidated financial statements is:

A $1,295,000

B $1,400,000

C $1,415,000

D̶ $1,425,000

850 + 650 + 25 (100) = 1,425

98 FR acquired 60% of the ordinary shares of TY on 1 January 20X1. The carrying amount of TY's net assets at 1 January 20X1 was $8.5m. The fair value of the net assets of TY was considered to be the same as their carrying amount with the following exception:

- an item of machinery had a carrying amount of $1.1m and its fair value was $1.75m. These assets were assessed to have a remaining useful life of 5 years from the date of acquisition.

FV adj 0.65   dep adj. 0.13)

FR is preparing the consolidated financial statements for the year-ended 31 December 20X1.   *$9.02 MM*

Which one of the following statements is true in respect of how the above would be reflected in FR's consolidated financial statements for the year ended 31 December 20X1?

A ✓ Additional depreciation of $130,000 would be charged in the consolidated statement of profit or loss ✓

B The machinery would be shown on the consolidated statement of financial position at $1.75m *1.75 - 0.13*

C The fair value adjustment ~~creates~~ *don't* a revaluation surplus of $650,000 *× They increase the net assets at acquisition ∴ increase goodwill*

D The fair value adjustment ~~has no impact~~ upon the group retained earnings ×
reduce parent's share of post acquisition profit held in group retained earnings

99 TF acquired 80% of the ordinary shares of JS on 1 January 20X1. The fair value of the net assets of JS was considered to be the same as their carrying amount with the following exception:

- JS had disclosed a contingent liability in the notes to its financial statements. Its fair value was considered to be $100,000 at acquisition and, at 31 December 20X1, was $110,000.

TF is preparing the consolidated financial statements for the year ended 31 December 20X1.

Which one of the following statements is true in respect of how the above would be reflected in TF's consolidated financial statements for the year ended 31 December 20X1?

A The contingent liability is ignored within the group accounts as the chances of it arising are not probable

B The contingent liability would be recognised as a liability of $100,000 in the consolidated statement of financial position × *$110,000*

C The increase in fair value of the contingent liability between acquisition and the reporting date should be recognised as a post-acquisition adjustment to ~~goodwill~~ *reserves (post acquisition profit)*

D̶ The contingent liability would increase the value of goodwill on acquisition.

OBJECTIVE TEST QUESTIONS : SECTION 1

100 MX acquired 80% of the 1 million issued $1 ordinary share capital of FZ on 1 April 20X9 for $1,750,000 when FZ's retained earnings were $920,000.

The carrying amount of FZ's net assets was considered to be the same as the fair value at the date of acquisition with the exception of FZ's machinery, which had a carrying amount of $680,000 and a fair value of $745,000 on 1 April 20X9. The remaining useful life of the machinery was estimated at 5 years from the date of acquisition.

MX depreciates all assets on a straight line basis over their estimated lives on a monthly basis.

The group policy is to measure non-controlling interest (NCI) at fair value at the date of acquisition. The fair value of the NCI at 1 April 20X9 was $320,000.

Calculate the carrying amount of goodwill that would be recognised in the consolidated statement of financial position of the MX Group at 31 December 20X9 (to the nearest $000).

$ __85__ 000

101 XM acquired 80% of the 1 million issued $1 ordinary share capital of ZF on 1 April 20X9 when ZF's retained earnings were $920,000.

A fair value adjustment on machinery of $65,000 arose at acquisition. The remaining useful life of the machinery was estimated at 5 years from the date of acquisition. XM depreciates all assets on a straight line basis over their estimated lives on a monthly basis.

ZF sold goods to XM with a sales value of $300,000 during the 9 months since the acquisition. All of these goods remain in XM's inventories at the reporting date. ZF makes 20% gross profit margin on all sales.

The retained earnings reported in the financial statements ZF as at 31 December 20X9 is $1.1 million.

The group policy is to measure non-controlling interest (NCI) at fair value at the date of acquisition. The fair value of the NCI at 1 April 20X9 was $320,000. There has been no impairment to goodwill since the date of acquisition.

The NCI to be included in the equity section of the consolidated statement of financial position of the XM group at 31 December 20X9 will be:

- A $341,400
- B $342,050
- C $354,050
- D $419,050

102 LJS acquired 80% of the 1 million issued $1 ordinary share capital of EMS on 1 April 20X9.

At acquisition a fair value adjustment of $130,000 arose. As a result, extra depreciation of $19,500 is included within the group accounts by the year end.

Since acquisition EMS sold goods to LJS and a provision for unrealised profit of £120,000 was required.

SUBJECT F2: ADVANCED FINANCIAL REPORTING

Which THREE of the following statements are true in respect of the consolidated retained earnings to be included in the consolidated statement of financial position of the LJS Group for the year ended 31 December 20X9?

A Group retained earnings will include 100% of LJS's retained earnings balance ✓

B 80% of EMS's post-acquisition earnings will be included as a debit (credit)

C The impact upon retained earnings caused by the unrealised profit adjustment will be $120,000   × 80% × 120,000

D The impact upon retained earnings caused by the fair value adjustment will be $15,600

E Both the unrealised profit adjustment and the fair value adjustment will cause a reduction to group retained earnings

103 JK acquired 75% of the 500,000 $1 equity shares of LM on 1 January 20X2 for $1,200,000 when the fair value of LM's net assets was $1,100,000. At the date of acquisition, the balance on LM's reserves was $350,000 and the only fair value adjustment required was in relation to a property with a remaining useful life at acquisition of ten years.

500,000
350,000
250,000 FV adj.
―――――
1,100,000

The carrying amount of property, plant and equipment in the individual financial statements of JK and LM at 31 December 20X2, the reporting date, are $3,300,000 and $850,000 respectively.

Calculate the carrying amount of property, plant and equipment that would be shown in the consolidated statement of financial position of the JK group at 31 December 20X2. State your answer to the nearest $000.

3,300,000
+ 850,000
――――――
4,150,000

4,150,000
+ 250,000
(25,000)
――――――
4,375,000

104 AB acquired an 80% investment in XY on 1 January 20X1. The consideration consisted of the following:

- The transfer of 500,000 shares in AB with a nominal value of $1.00 each and a market value on the date of acquisition of $3.50 each
- $408,000 of cash paid on 1 January 20X1; and
- $1,000,000 of cash, payable on 1 January 20X3 (a discount rate of 9% has been used to value the liability in the financial statements of AB).

AB also paid legal and professional fees in respect of the acquisition of $150,000.

The best estimate of the fair value of the consideration to be included in the calculation of goodwill arising on the acquisition of XY is:

A $1,750,000   500,000 × $3.50 = 1,750,000
B $3,000,000   = 408,000
C $3,150,000   VP 1MM m 2 9% = 841,679
D $3,158,000   ――――――
                                  2,999,679 ≈ 3,000,000

105 AB acquired 80% of CD's 500,000 ordinary shares for $620,000 on 1 January 20X7 when the fair value of CD's net assets was $680,000. The market price of CD's ordinary shares at 1 January 20X7 was $1.80.

Net assets.

The directors of AB are trying to decide whether to measure the non-controlling interest of CD at fair value or the proportionate share of the fair value of net assets at acquisition.

Calculate the ADDITIONAL goodwill that would be recognised if the directors choose the fair value method over the proportionate method. State your answer to the nearest $.

Proportion : PP = 620,000   FV = PP = 620,000
method   NCi 680,000 × 20%   NCi = 100,000 × 1.80
           NetA (680,000)   NA (680,000)
           ――――――   ――――――
           GW $76,000   GW 120,000

30

OBJECTIVE TEST QUESTIONS : SECTION 1

106 ZB acquired 70% of the 1 million issued $1 ordinary shares of HD on 1 January 20X3 for $3,250,000 when HD's retained earnings were $1,500,000. ZB has no other subsidiaries.

The carrying amount of HD's net assets was considered to be the same as the fair value at the date of acquisition with the exception of HD's non-depreciable property. The carrying amount of these assets was $1,200,000 and the fair value was $1,600,000.

The group policy is to measure non-controlling interest at fair value at the acquisition date. The fair value of the non-controlling interest in HD was $1,325,000 on 1 January 20X3.

An impairment review performed on 31 December 20X4 indicated that goodwill on the acquisition of HD had been impaired by $425,000. No impairment was recognised in the year ended 31 December 20X3. The retained earnings of HD at 31 December 20X4 were $2,750,000.

The goodwill that will be recorded in non-current assets of the ZB group as at 31 December 20X4 is:

- A $795,000
- B $1,250,000
- C $1,650,000
- D $1,675,000

107 BZ acquired 70% of the 1 million issued $1 ordinary shares of DH on 1 January 20X3 for $3,250,000 when DH's retained earnings were $1,500,000. BZ has no other subsidiaries.

A fair value uplift of $400,000 on DH's non-depreciable property is included in DH's net assets at acquisition.

The group policy is to measure non-controlling interest at fair value at the acquisition date.

An impairment review performed on 31 December 20X4 indicated that goodwill on the acquisition of DH had been impaired by $850,000.

Which of the following statements are INCORRECT in respect of the consolidated retained earnings of the BZ group at 31 December 20X4?

- A   70% of DH's post-acquisition retained earnings will be credited to it
- B   100% of BZ's retained earnings will be included in it
- C   It will be affected by the fair value adjustment arising at the date of acquisition
- D   Goodwill impairment of $595,000 will be deducted in it

108 LB acquired 70% of the 1 million issued $1 ordinary shares of NB on 1 January 20X3 for $3,250,000 when NB's retained earnings were $1,500,000. LB has no other subsidiaries.

The carrying amount of NB's net assets was considered to be the same as the fair value.

The group policy is to measure non-controlling interest at fair value at the acquisition date. The fair value of the non-controlling interest in NB was $1,325,000 on 1 January 20X3.

An impairment review performed on 31 December 20X4 indicated that goodwill on the acquisition of NB had been impaired by $425,000. No impairment was recognised in the year ended 31 December 20X3. The retained earnings of NB at 31 December 20X4 were $2,750,000.

SUBJECT F2: ADVANCED FINANCIAL REPORTING

The non-controlling interest to be included in the consolidated statement of financial position of the LB group at 31 December 20X4 will be:

A $1,117,500

B $1,245,000

C $1,572,500 ✓

D $1,700,000

NCI at acq. 1,325,000
+ (2750 − 1500k) × 30%
− 425,000 × 30%
―――――――
1,572,500

109 BC acquired 65% of the ordinary share capital of FG, its only subsidiary, on 1 January 20X3. In the year ended 31 December 20X3, FG had total comprehensive income of $125,000. A fair value adjustment at acquisition resulted in additional depreciation of $30,000 being charged to consolidated profit or loss in the year ended 31 December 20X3.

The directors of BC carried out an impairment review on the goodwill arising on the acquisition of FG at 31 December 20X3 and considered it to have been impaired by $15,000.

It is group policy to measure non-controlling interest at fair value at the date of acquisition.

What is the affect upon consolidated reserves of the BC group caused by FG as at 31 December 20X3?

A $52,000 ✓

B $61,750

C $71,500

D $81,250

125,000
(30,000)
(15,000) × 65%
―――――――
80,000 × 65%

110 Which THREE of the following statements are true in respect of the recognition of non-controlling interests in consolidated financial statements?

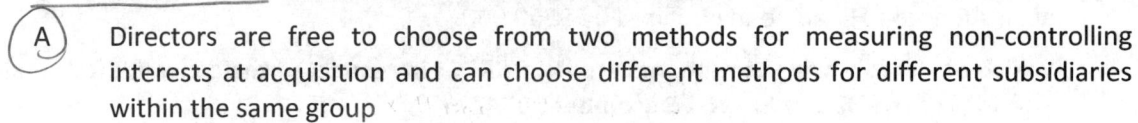

A ○ Directors are free to choose from two methods for measuring non-controlling interests at acquisition and can choose different methods for different subsidiaries within the same group

B   Goodwill impairment will always affect the non-controlling interest , *just when is FV method*

C   Provisions for unrealised profits on transactions between entities within the same group will always affect the non-controlling interest *net asset △*
↳ just when S to P

D ○ The non-controlling interest is initially recognised at acquisition by debiting goodwill and crediting equity

E   The non-controlling interest's share of any dividend paid by a subsidiary ~~is eliminated upon consolidation~~ *will be reflected in the statement of changes in equity. It is the parents share that would be eliminated upon consolidation.*

F ○ The non-controlling interest will always be reduced by their share of any additional depreciation charge arising from fair value adjustments to a subsidiary's non-current assets at acquisition

OBJECTIVE TEST QUESTIONS : SECTION 1

111 AB acquired 80% of the ordinary share capital of CD, its only subsidiary, on 1 October 20X8. In the year ended 30 June 20X9, CD had total comprehensive income of $90,000. A fair value adjustment at acquisition resulted in additional depreciation of $20,000 being charged to profit or loss in the year ended 30 June 20X9.

The directors of AB carried out an impairment review on the goodwill arising on the acquisition of CD at 30 June 20X9 and considered it to have been impaired by $30,000.

AB sold goods to CD on 1 May 20X9 with a sales value of $80,000. Half of these goods remain in CD's inventories at 30 June 20X9. AB makes a 25% gross profit margin on all sales. *[handwritten: P to S / Non adj for NCI / Parents made the profit not NCI]*

It is group policy to measure non-controlling interest at fair value at the date of acquisition. Profit is assumed to accrue evenly throughout the year.

The share of total comprehensive income attributable to the non-controlling interest for the year ended 30 June 20X9 is:

A $1,500
B $3,500   *(circled)*
C $6,000
D $8,000

*[handwritten working:
Profit attributable to NCI:
67,500 → 90000 × 9/12
($20,000) → depreciation
($30,000) → goodwill
$17,500 × 20% = $3,500]*

112 PA owns 80% of the ordinary share capital of SU, its only subsidiary. It is group policy to measure non-controlling interest at fair value at the date of acquisition.

When calculating the total comprehensive income attributable to the non-controlling interest each year, the subsidiary's profit must be adjusted for which of the following transactions?

Select ALL that apply.

A   Profit on the sale of goods by PA to SU, where SU still holds the goods at the reporting date *[handwritten: not attributable to NCI because just reduce PA profit]*

B   Profit on the sale of goods by SU to PA, where PA still holds the goods at the reporting date *(circled)* *[handwritten: reduce SU profit therefore NCI and PA profit]*

C   Impairment to the goodwill arising on the acquisition of SU ✓

D   Additional depreciation arising from a fair value adjustment made to SU's net assets at the date of acquisition ✓

E   Elimination of dividend paid by SU to PA *[handwritten: same above]*

113 SA acquired 75% of the ordinary shares of TR on 1 August 20X3 for $2,200,000. At the date of acquisition, the carrying amount of TR's net assets was $1,220,000 and this was considered to be equal to the fair value with the exception of property, plant and equipment. The fair value of property, plant and equipment was $475,000 higher than its carrying amount and had an estimated useful life of 20 years from the date of acquisition. TR is SA's only subsidiary.

It is group policy to measure non-controlling interest at its proportionate share of the fair value of the net assets at the date of acquisition.

The carrying amount of TR's net assets at the reporting date of 31 July 20X7 is $2,500,000.

Goodwill arising on the acquisition of TR had been impaired by $150,000 at 31 July 20X7.

Calculate the non-controlling interest in the consolidated statement of financial position of the SA group as at 31 July 20X7. State your answer to the nearest $.

*[handwritten at bottom:
NCI at acq = 1,695,000 × 25% = 423,750
(2,500,000
− 1,220,000
− 95,000) → dep   × 25% = 296,250
720,000]*

SUBJECT F2: ADVANCED FINANCIAL REPORTING

114 ER acquired 80% of the equity share capital of MR on 1 January 20X0 for $2,000,000 when the retained earnings of MR were $1,200,000. At the date of acquisition, the fair value of the net assets of MR was the same as the carrying amount with the exception of property, plant and equipment. The fair value of property, plant and equipment was $400,000 higher than its carrying amount. Property, plant and equipment had an estimated useful life of 10 years from the date of acquisition.

The carrying amount of property, plant and equipment in the individual financial statements of ER and MR at 31 December 20X2, the reporting date, were $5,900,000 and $2,000,000 respectively.

Calculate the carrying amount of property, plant and equipment that would be presented in the consolidated statement of financial position of the ER Group as at 31 December 20X2.

Give your answer to the nearest $000.

115 YG acquired 75% of the ordinary share capital of VB, its only subsidiary, on 1 July 20X6. In the year ended 31 December 20X6, VB made total profit of $180,000. A fair value adjustment at acquisition resulted in additional depreciation of $15,000 being charged to profit or loss in the post-acquisition period.

VB sold goods to YG on 1 November 20X6 with a sales value of $100,000. 30% of these goods remain in YG's inventories at 31 December 20X6. VB makes a 30% gross profit margin on all sales.

The directors carried out an impairment review on the goodwill arising on the acquisition of VB at 31 December 20X6 and charged $25,000 to consolidated profit or loss as a result.

It is group policy to measure non-controlling interest at the proportionate share of the fair value of net assets at the date of acquisition. Profit is assumed to accrue evenly throughout the year.

The profit attributable to the non-controlling interest for the year ended 31 December 20X6 is:

A $10,250
B $12,500
C $16,500
D $18,750

116 At 1 January 20X8, Tom acquired 80% of the share capital of Jerry for $100,000. At that date the share capital of Jerry consisted of 50,000 $1 ordinary shares and its reserves were $30,000. The carrying amount of Jerry's net assets was the same as the fair value as at the acquisition date.

At 31 December 20X9, the reserves of Tom and Jerry were as follows:

Tom $400,000

Jerry $50,000

Goodwill impairment at 31 December 20X9 is assumed to be 60% of the goodwill at the date of acquisition. NCI is valued using the proportion of net assets method.

What is group reserves in Tom's consolidated statement of financial position at 31 December 20X9?

A $394,400
B $398,720
C $416,000
D $428,400

117 HB sold goods to S2, its 100% owned subsidiary, on 1 November 20X8. The goods were sold to S2 for $33,000. HB made a profit of 25% on the original cost of the goods.

At the year-end, 31 March 20X9, 50% of the goods had been sold by S2. The remaining goods were included in S2's inventory.

Which of the following statements illustrate the correct treatment for the adjustment required to inventory in the HB consolidated financial statements at 31 March 20X9?

A   Reduce inventory by $3,300   Increase cost of sales by $3,300
B   Increase inventory by $8,250 Reduce cost of sales by $8,250
C   Reduce inventory by $6,600   Increase cost of sales by $6,600
D   Reduce inventory by $4,125   Reduce cost of sales by $4,125

118 During the year Fluff sold goods at $168,000 to its 90% owned subsidiary Ball. These goods were sold at a mark-up of 50% on cost. On 31 December, Ball still had $36,000 worth of these goods in inventory.

Which of the following statements are true?

Select all that apply

A   In the statement of financial position, an adjustment of $56,000 will be processed by reducing group retained earnings and inventory

B   An increase to cost of sales of $12,000 is required within the statement of profit or loss

C   The non-controlling interest will take a 90% share of the required PUP adjustment

D   Group's revenue and cost of sales will be reduced by $36,000

SUBJECT F2: ADVANCED FINANCIAL REPORTING

119 ZY purchased 80% of the equity shares in XW on 1 October 20X2.

ZY and XW trade with each other. During the year ended 30 September 20X3, ZY sold XW inventory at a sales price of $50,000. All of these goods remained in XW's inventory. ZY applied a mark-up on cost of 25%.

Extracts from the statement of profit or loss of the two entities are shown below:

	ZY $000	XW $000
Revenue	1,000	750
Cost of sales	(650)	(250)

What would be the revenue and cost of sales figures reported within the ZY consolidated statement of profit or loss for the year ended 30 September 20X3?

	Revenue $000	Cost of sales $000
A	950	600
B	1,700	850
C	1,700	860
D	1,750	900

120 YZ purchased 80% of the equity shares in WX on 1 October 20X2.

YZ and WX trade with each other. At 30 September 20X3, WX held an outstanding payable balance of $10,000 to YZ. This was after accounting for cash of $5,000 paid on 29 September 20X9. YZ is yet to receive the cash.

What journal entry would correctly record the adjustment for the intra-group outstanding balance in the consolidated financial statements?

A Dr Payable $15,000   Cr Receivable $10,000
                         Cr Cash $5,000

B Dr Cash $5,000
   Dr Payable $5,000   Cr Receivable $10,000

C Dr Cash $5,000
   Dr Payable $10,000   Cr Receivable $15,000

D Dr Payables $10,000   Cr Receivable $10,000

OBJECTIVE TEST QUESTIONS : SECTION 1

121 Josh Co purchased 80% of the equity shares in Homme Co on 1 October 20X2.

Josh Co and Homme Co trade with each other. During the year ended 30 September 20X3, Josh Co sold Homme Co inventory at a sales price of $28,000. Josh Co applied a mark-up on cost of 33.33%.

Homme Co still held $6,000 of the goods purchased from Josh Co in its inventory as at the year end.

What is the correct journal entry to record the adjustment for the PUP in the consolidated financial statements?

A   Dr Inventory $1,500   Cr Cost of sales $1,500

B   Dr Cost of sales $1,500   Cr Inventory $1,500

C   Dr inventory $2,000   Cr Cost of sales $2,000

D   Dr Cost of sales $2,000   Dr inventory $2,000

122 Which one of the following is not included within the definition of control per IFRS 10 *Consolidated Financial Statements*?

A   Having power over the investee

B   Having exposure, or rights, to variable returns from its investment with the investee

C   Having the majority of shares in the investee

D   Having the ability to use its power over the investee to affect the amount of the investor's returns

123 IFRS Standards require extensive use of fair values when recording the acquisition of a subsidiary.

Which TWO of the following statements, regarding the use of fair values on the acquisition of a subsidiary, are correct?

A   The use of fair value to record a subsidiary's acquired assets does not comply with the historical cost principle.

B   The use of fair values to record the acquisition of plant always increases consolidated post-acquisition depreciation charges compared to the corresponding charge in the subsidiary's own financial statements.

C   Cash consideration payable one year after the date of acquisition needs to be discounted to reflect its fair value.

D   When acquiring a subsidiary, the fair value of liabilities and contingent liabilities must also be considered.

SUBJECT F2: ADVANCED FINANCIAL REPORTING

124 On 30 June 20X4, GHI acquired 800,000 of JKL's 1 million shares. *[80%]*

GHI issued 3 shares for every 4 shares acquired in JKL. On 30 June 20X4, the market price of a GHI share was $3.80 and the market price of a JKL share was $3. *[600,000 shares × MP GHI]*

GHI agreed to pay $550,000 in cash to the existing shareholders on 30 June 20X5. GHI's borrowing rate was 10% per annum. *[PV = $500,000]*

GHI paid professional fees of $100,000 for advice on the acquisition. *→ expense*

What is the cost of investment that will be used in the goodwill calculation in the consolidated financial statements of GHI? Give your answer to the nearest $000.

$ __2,780__ ,000

ASSOCIATES AND JOINT ARRANGEMENTS

125 Complete the following sentences by placing one of the options identified below in each of the spaces.

arrangement	entity
operation	venture

A joint __arrangement__ is an arrangement in which two parties or more have joint control.

A joint __operation__ is where the parties that have joint control have rights to the assets, and obligations for the liabilities, relating to the arrangement.

A joint __venture__ is where the parties that have joint control have rights to the net assets of the arrangement.

126 XZ owns 35% of the equity share capital of TY. During the year to 31 December 20X1, XZ purchased goods with a sales value of $200,000 from TY. Half of these goods remained in XZ's inventories at the year ended 31 December 20X1. TY makes a gross profit margin of 25% on all sales. *[stop]*

Which of the following accounting adjustments would XZ process in the preparation of its consolidated financial statements in relation to these goods?

A	Dr Share of profit of associate	$7,000	Cr	Inventories	$7,000
B	Dr Cost of sales	$7,000	Cr	Investment in associate	$7,000
C ✓	Dr Share of profit of associate	$8,750	Cr	Inventories	$8,750
D	Dr Cost of sales	$8,750	Cr	Investment in associate	$8,750

200,000 sale.
50% inventory
100,000 sale.

25,000 profit × 35% = 8,750

OBJECTIVE TEST QUESTIONS : SECTION 1

127 Brendan bought 30% of WeeJoe on 1 July 20X4. Brendan is deemed to exert significant influence over WeeJoe and already owns other investments in subsidiaries. WeeJoe's statement of profit or loss for the year shows a profit of $600,000. WeeJoe paid a dividend to Brendan of $75,000 on 1 December 20X4. → Not in P&L

Since the 1 July 20X4, WeeJoe has sold goods to Brendan with a sales value of $25,000. WeeJoe uses a mark-up on cost of 25%. By the year end, 20% of these goods have been sold on by Brendan.

At the year end, the investment in WeeJoe was judged to have been impaired by $15,000.

What is the 'Share of profit from associate' in Brendan's consolidated statement of profit or loss for the year ended 31 December 20X4?

A	$71,000
B	$73,800
C	$75,000
D	$86,000
E	$165,000

Handwritten working:
- 600,000 × 6/12 = 300,000
- (4,000)
- 296,000 × 0.3 = 88,800
- (15,000) impairment
- 73,800 ✓
- 20,000 / 125%
- (16,000) / 100%
- 4,000

128 Dolph bought 20% of Chuck on 1 January 20X8, when Chuck had $1 ordinary share capital of $1,000,000 and $4,000,000 retained earnings. Dolph exerts significant influence over Chuck and already prepares consolidated accounts.

Dolph paid by giving the previous owners of Chuck, 1 Dolph share for every 4 shares bought in Chuck. At the date of acquisition, Dolph's shares had a market value of $4.50 and Chuck's had a market value of $2. (1D : 4C)

At 31 December 20X8, Chuck's net assets were $4,600,000. At the year-end, Dolph considered the investment in Chuck to be impaired by $100,000.

During the year, Dolph sells goods at a price of $200,000 to Chuck making a total profit of $50,000. All of these goods remain in the inventory of Chuck as at the year-end. (P to S)

What is the 'Investment in associate' in the consolidated statement of financial position as at 31 December 20X8?

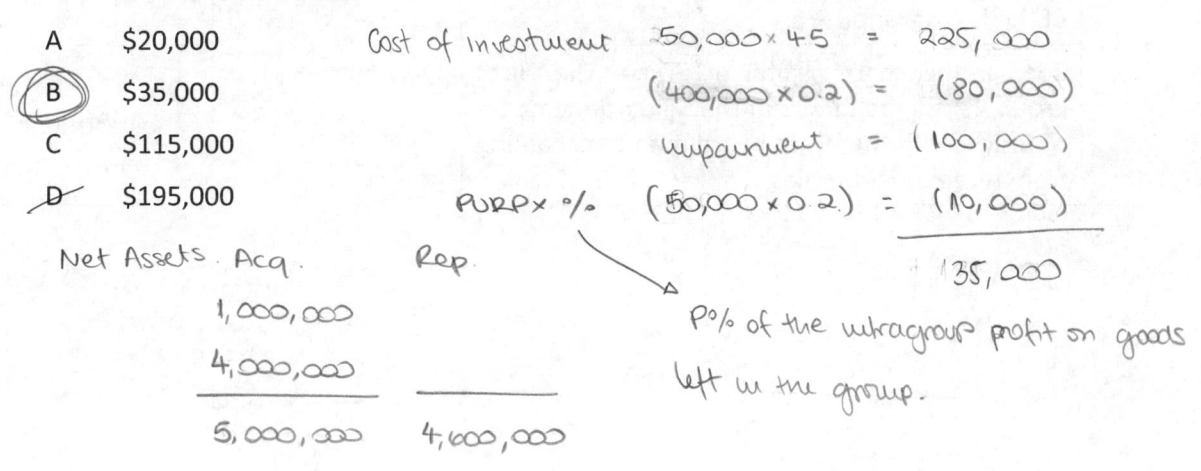

A	$20,000
B	$35,000
C	$115,000
D	$195,000

Handwritten working:
- Cost of investment: 50,000 × 4.5 = 225,000
- (400,000 × 0.2) = (80,000)
- impairment = (100,000)
- PURP × % (50,000 × 0.2) = (10,000)
- 35,000

Net Assets:
Acq.	Rep.
1,000,000	
4,000,000	
5,000,000	4,600,000

P% of the intragroup profit on goods left in the group.

39

SUBJECT F2: ADVANCED FINANCIAL REPORTING

129 The HC group acquired 30% of the equity share capital of AF on 1 April 20X8 paying $25,000.

At 1 April 20X8, the equity section of AF's statement of financial position comprised:

	$
$1 equity shares	50,000
Share premium	12,500
Retained earnings	10,000

AF made a profit for the year to 31 March 20X9 (prior to dividend distribution) of $6,500 and paid a dividend of $3,500 to its equity shareholders.

Calculate the value of HC's investment in AF for inclusion in HC's consolidated statement of financial position at 31 March 20X9.

$ __25,900__

Handwritten working:
Cost of investment 25,000
Profit after dividends 900 ((6,500 − 3,500) × 30%)
25,900

130 AB owns 40% of CD. During the year the investment in CD suffered impairment of $1,000. How should the impairment be treated in the consolidated financial statements?

- A Increase the operating expenses by $1,000
- **B** Reduce the share of the associate's profit by $1,000
- C Increase the operating expenses by $400
- D Reduce the share of the associate's profit by $400

131 Identify the correct treatments for the following investments in the consolidated financial statements of the Nicol group.

30% of the share capital of Hansen. The other 70% is owned by Lawro, another listed entity, whose directors make up Hansen's board.	Subsidiary > 50%
80% of the share capital of Kennedy, whose activities are significantly different from the rest of the Nicol group.	Associate — significant influence [20% − 50%]
30% of the share capital of Bruce. The Nicol group have appointed 2 of the 5 board members of Bruce, with the other board members coming from three other entities.	Investment

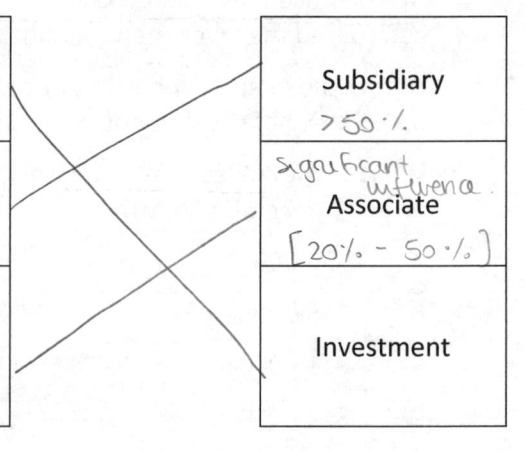

40

OBJECTIVE TEST QUESTIONS : SECTION 1

132 Green is an associate undertaking of Purple. Purple owns 30% of the shares in Green, and has done so for many years.

During the year ended 31 December 20X4, Green made a net profit of $1.5 million. Green sold goods to Purple during the year with a value of $2 million, and half are still in Purple's inventories at the year end. All the goods were sold at a margin of 30%.

Purple has recognised previous impairments in relation to its investment in Green of $225,000. In the current year, Purple wishes to recognise an additional impairment charge of $35,000.

What is the share of profit of associate to be shown in Purple's consolidated statement of profit or loss?

$ _____235_____ ,000

133 'An associate is an entity over which the investor has significant influence' (IAS28, para 3).

Which TWO of the following indicate the presence of significant influence?

- (A) The investor owns 330,000 of the 1,500,000 equity voting shares of the investee
- (B) The investor has representation on the board of directors of the investee ✓
- C The investor is able to insist that all of the sales of the investee are made to a subsidiary of the investor
- D The investor controls the votes of a majority of the board members ✓

134 Virgil paid $1.2 million for a 30% investment in Dijk's equity shares on 1 August 20X4.

Dijk's profit after tax for the year ended 31 March 20X5 was $750,000. On 31 March 20X5, Dijk had $300,000 goods in its inventory which it had bought from Virgil in March 20X5. These had been sold by Virgil at a mark-up on cost of 20%.

Dijk has not paid any dividends.

On the assumption that Dijk is an associate of Virgil, what would be the carrying amount of the investment in Dijk in the consolidated statement of financial position of Virgil as at 31 March 20X5?

$ _____1,335_____ ,000

135 Complete the following sentence using the options provided within the table.

To consolidate an associated investment, the group would _not consolidate_ the assets and liabilities of the associate and _wouldn't eliminate_ any outstanding intra-group balances between the parent and the associate.

not consolidate	100% consolidate
eliminate	would not eliminate

SUBJECT F2: ADVANCED FINANCIAL REPORTING

CONSOLIDATED STATEMENT OF CASH FLOWS AND CSOCIE

136 Select, from the list below, **THREE** items that would be included in the 'cash flows from operating activities' section of the consolidated statement of cash flows.

- A   Cash paid upon acquisition of a subsidiary, net of cash acquired
- B   Cash paid upon acquisition of intangible assets
- C   Dividends received from associate
- D   Gain on sale of subsidiary
- E   Goodwill impairment
- F   Share of associate's profit for the year

137 In a consolidated statement of cash flows, which **TWO** of the following would be included in cash flows from investing activities of the group?

- A   Dividend received from an associate
- B   Gain on disposal of property, plant and equipment
- C   Cash paid on the acquisition of an associate
- D   Share of associate's other comprehensive income
- E   Share of associate's profit or loss

138 DF's consolidated statement of financial position shows inventories with a carrying amount of $34,800,000 at 31 December 20X2 and $36,000,000 at 31 December 20X1.

DF acquired all of the share capital of SD on 1 October 20X2, when the carrying amount of the inventories in SD was $3,600,000.

The adjustment caused by the movement in inventories within cash flows from operating activities for the year ended 31 December 20X2 is:

- A $2,400,000 deduction
- B $2,400,000 addition
- C $4,800,000 deduction
- D $4,800,000 addition

139 MIC's consolidated statement of financial position shows property, plant and equipment with a carrying amount of $16,800,000 at 31 March 20X7 and $15,600,000 at 31 March 20X6.

There were no disposals of property, plant and equipment in the year. Depreciation charged in arriving at profit totalled $1,800,000. MIC acquired an 80% holding in GH on 1 December 20X6 for $4 million. The fair value of the property, plant and equipment in GH at 1 December 20X6 was $800,000.

Calculate the cash outflow from the purchase of property, plant and equipment included in the consolidated statement of cash flows of the MIC Group for the year ended 31 March 20X7.

Give your answer to the nearest $000.

140 An extract from AB's consolidated statement of financial position at 31 December 20X1 is as follows:

	20X1	20X0
	$000	$000
Equity attributable to owners of the parent:		
Non-controlling interests	19,500	18,300

An extract from AB's consolidated statement of profit or loss and other comprehensive income for the year ended 31 December 20X1 is as follows:

Profit for the year attributable to:	$000
Owners of the parent	3,880
Non-controlling interests	610
	4,490

Total comprehensive income attributable to:	
Owners of the parent	5,130
Non-controlling interests	680
	5,810

AB acquired 70% of the ordinary share capital of XY on 1 January 20X1 when XY's net assets had a fair value of $4,400,000. The group policy is to value the NCI at acquisition at its proportionate share of the fair value of the net assets. There were no other purchases or sales of investments in the year.

The dividends paid to the NCI that would appear in the cash flows from financing activities section of the consolidated statement of cash flows of the AB Group for the year ended 30 June 20X1 is:

A $520,000
B $730,000
C $800,000
D $3,200,000

(handwritten working:)
NCi b/f   1,320 + 18,300
NCi + CI   680
NCi c/f   (19,500)

141 An extract from AB's consolidated statement of financial position at 31 December 20X1 is as follows:

	20X1	20X0
	$000	$000
Equity attributable to owners of the parent:		
Revaluation surplus	1,250	–
Retained earnings	21,850	20,100

(handwritten working:)
20,100
3,880 → Profit
(21,850)
2,130

An extract from AB's consolidated statement of profit or loss and other comprehensive income for the year ended 31 December 20X1 is as follows:

	$000
Profit for the year attributable to:	
Owners of the parent	3,880
Non-controlling interests	610
	4,490
Total comprehensive income attributable to:	
Owners of the parent	5,130
Non-controlling interests	680
	5,810

Calculate the dividends paid to the parent shareholders that would appear in the cash flows from financing activities section of the consolidated statement of cash flows of the AB Group for the year ended 30 June 20X1. State your answer to the nearest $000.

142 GH's consolidated statement of financial position shows an investment in associate of $6,200,000 at 30 June 20X2 and $5,700,000 at 30 June 20X1. There were no acquisitions or disposals of associates in the year ended 30 June 20X2.

GH's share of associate's profit for the year ended 30 June 20X2 was $1,800,000. The share of associate's other comprehensive income was $200,000.

The dividends received from associate that would appear in the cash flows from investing activities section of the consolidated statement of cash flows of the GH Group for the year ended 30 June 20X2 is:

A $1,100,000
B $1,500,000
C $2,100,000
D $2,500,000

143 BC's consolidated statement of financial position shows a carrying amount of goodwill of $8 million at 31 May 20X1 and $7.2 million at 31 May 20X0.

BC acquired 70% of the ordinary share capital of YZ on 1 January 20X1 for a cash consideration of $500,000 plus the issue of 1 million $1 ordinary shares in BC, which had a deemed value of $3.95 per share at the date of acquisition. The fair values of the net assets acquired on 1 January 20X1 were $4.4 million.

The group policy is to value the non-controlling interests at acquisition at its proportionate share of the fair value of the net assets.

The goodwill impairment that would be reflected as an adjustment from profit to net cash from operations in the consolidated statement of cash flows of the BC Group for the year ended 31 May 20X1 is:

A $570,000

B $750,000

C $800,000

D $2,170,000

144 Imran purchased 80% of the equity shares in Shoaib on 1 October 20X2.

Extracts from the statement of changes in equity of the two entities are shown below:

	Imran $000	Shoaib $000
Equity b/f	7,500	5,000
Total comprehensive income	650	250

What would be the total comprehensive income figure attributable to parent shareholders reported within the consolidated statement of changes in equity for the year ended 30 September 20X3? All options are presented to the nearest $000s.

A 650

B 700

C 850

D 900

145 CardiB purchased 90% of the equity shares in Stormzy on 1 January 20X1.

Extracts from the statement of changes in equity of the two entities are shown below:

	CardiB $000	Stormzy $000
Equity b/f	3,500	2,000
Total comprehensive income	350	250
Dividends paid	(100)	(100)

What would be the total comprehensive income attributable to the NCI and the dividend paid to NCIs reported within the consolidated statement of changes in equity for the year ended 31 December 20X2? All options are presented to the nearest $000s.

	Total comprehensive income attributable to NCI $000	Dividend paid to NCI $000
A	25	10
B	35	10
C	60	100
D	250	100

SUBJECT F2: ADVANCED FINANCIAL REPORTING

FOREIGN CURRENCY CONSOLIDATIONS

146 IAS® 21 *The effects of changes in foreign exchange rates* governs the translation of foreign operations.

Which TWO of the following statements are true in respect of foreign subsidiaries and their treatment in consolidated financial statements?

- A Exchange differences arising on the translation of a foreign operation are recognised in the statement of profit or loss ✗
- B Goodwill should be translated in the consolidated statement of financial position at the closing rate
- C Subsidiaries are required to present financial statements in the presentation currency of the parent ✗
- D The exchange difference arising on translation of goodwill is always allocated between parent shareholders and non-controlling interest
- E The exchange difference arising on translation of net assets is always allocated between parent shareholders and non-controlling interest

147 FG acquired 100% of the ordinary share capital of KL on 1 August 20X4 for 204,000 Crowns. KL's share capital at that date comprised 1,000 ordinary shares of 1 Crown each and its reserves were 180,000 Crowns. The carrying amount of KL's net assets was considered to be the same as fair value.

FG's directors conducted an impairment review of the goodwill at 31 July 20X5 and concluded that goodwill had lost 10% of its value during the year as a result of losses made by the subsidiary.

FG presents its consolidated financial statements in $.

The relevant exchange rates are as follows:

1 August 20X4	$1=1.7 Crowns
31 July 20X5	$1=2.2 Crowns
Average rate for the year ended 31 July 20X5	$1=1.9 Crowns

Calculate the value of goodwill that will be presented in FG's consolidated financial statements at 31 July 20X5 in $ to the nearest whole number.

148 A acquired 80% of the equity share capital of B on 1 January 20X1. A's presentational and functional currency is the A$. B presents its financial statements in the B$. It is group policy to value the non-controlling interest at the proportionate share of the fair value of the net assets.

The A group's consolidated statement of profit or loss and other comprehensive income for the year ended 31 December 20X1 includes the following exchange difference arising on the translation of B:

	A$000
Exchange loss on translation of B	
On goodwill	(100)
On net assets	(50)
Total exchange loss for year	(150)

B's profit for the year was B$800,000 and it had no other comprehensive income.

Relevant exchange rates are as follows:

1 January 20X1	A$1=B$2.00
31 December 20X1	A$1=B$2.30
Average rate for the year ended 31 December 20X1	A$1=B$2.10

The total comprehensive income attributable to the non-controlling interest in A Group's consolidated statement of profit or loss and other comprehensive income for the year ended 31 December 20X1 is:

A   A$ 46,190

B   A$ 56,190

C   A$ 66,190

D   A$ 86,290

149 Place the following options into the highlighted boxes in the table below to correctly calculate the annual exchange difference on translation of a foreign subsidiary's net assets:

acquisition rate
average rate for the year
closing rate
opening rate
Less: net assets at acquisition at
Less: opening net assets at

Exchange difference on net assets		$
Closing net assets at	closing rate	X
Less: comprehensive income at	average rate	(X)
opening net assets	opening rate	(X)
		____
Exchange difference on net assets for the year		X
		____

150 HM acquired 80% of the ordinary share capital of a foreign entity, OS, on 1 January 20X1 for Crowns 13,984,000. At the date of acquisition, the net assets of OS had a fair value of Crowns 15,800,000. The group policy is to value non-controlling interest (NCI) at fair value at the date of acquisition. The fair value of the NCI at the date of acquisition was Crowns 3,496,000. At 31 December 20X1, the goodwill that arose on the acquisition of OS was impaired by 20%. Impairment is translated at the average rate and is charged to group administrative expenses.

HM presents its consolidated financial statements in $.

The relevant exchange rates are as follows:

1 January 20X1	$1=1.61 Crowns
31 December 20X1	$1=1.52 Crowns
Average rate for the year ended 31 December 20X1	$1=1.58 Crowns

47

SUBJECT F2: ADVANCED FINANCIAL REPORTING

Calculate the exchange difference arising on the translation of goodwill that will be included in HM's consolidated statement of other comprehensive income for the year ended 31 December 20X1.

Give your answer to the nearest $000.

151 BC acquired 75% of the equity share capital of DE on 1 January 20X1. BC's presentational and functional currency is the $. DE presents its financial statements in the dinar. At the date of acquisition, the carrying amount of DE's assets was considered to be the same as fair value.

The carrying amount of DE's net assets in its financial statements at 31 December 20X3 is 3,800,000 dinars and its comprehensive income for the year was 1,350,000.

Relevant exchange rates are as follows:

1 January 20X1	$1=25 dinar
31 December 20X2	$1=36 dinar
31 December 20X3	$1=32 dinar
Average rate for the year ended 31 December 20X3	$1=35 dinar

The exchange difference arising on the translation of the net assets of DE to be presented in the BC Group's statement of other comprehensive income for the year ended 31 December 20X3 is:

- A $9,092 gain
- B $9,092 loss
- C $12,123 gain
- D $12,123 loss

152 The functional currency of A is the A$. On 1 October 20X2, A acquired 80% of B for A$5,200,000. B presents its financial statements in the B$. The fair value of B's net assets at the date of acquisition was B$2,800,000.

The group policy is to value the non-controlling interest (NCI) at fair value at the date of acquisition. The fair value of the NCI of B at 1 October 20X2 was B$600,000.

There has been no impairment of goodwill since the date of acquisition.

Relevant exchange rates are as follows:

1 October 20X2	A$1=B$0.50
30 September 20X3	A$1=B$0.71
Average rate for the year ended 30 September 20X3	A$1=B$0.65

The goodwill on the acquisition of B in the consolidated statement of financial position of the A Group at 30 September 20X3 is:

- A A$ 400,000
- B A$ 563,380
- C A$ 615,385
- D A$ 800,000

153 GD acquired 70% of the ordinary share capital of WR on 1 July 20X3 for $2,400,000. GD's functional and presentation currency is the $ and WR's presentation currency is the groat (Gr).

At the date of acquisition, the carrying amount of WR's net assets was Gr 5,800,000 and this was the same as fair value with the exception of some property that had a fair value considered to be Gr 500,000 greater than its carrying amount. The property had a remaining useful life of 40 years at acquisition.

The carrying amount of property, plant and equipment of GD and WR at 30 June 20X6 was $12,800,000 and Gr 4,300,000 respectively.

Relevant exchange rates are as follows:

1 July 20X3	$1=Gr 2.9
30 June 20X5	$1=Gr 3.7
30 June 20X6	$1=Gr 4.1
Average rate for the year ended 30 June 20X6	$1=Gr 3.9

The carrying amount of property, plant and equipment in the consolidated statement of financial position of the GD group at 30 June 20X6, to the nearest $, is:

- A $13,848,780
- B $13,961,585
- C $13,967,683
- D $14,021,154

154 BH prepares its financial statements in dollars, its functional currency, and is considering acquiring 80% of the equity share capital of NJ.

NJ is based overseas in a country that uses the Kron as its currency. NJ sources all its raw materials locally, recruits a local workforce and is subject to local taxes and corporate regulations. Most of its sales are to customers in other countries.

If the acquisition goes ahead, NJ will continue to operate relatively autonomously within the group and will raise its own finance locally.

Which of the following statements are true?

Select ALL that apply.

A   NJ will be a subsidiary of BH and should, therefore, select the dollar as its functional currency to match with its parent, BH.

B   The functional currency of NJ will be determined by the currency that dominates the primary economic environment in which NJ operates

C   The functional currency of NJ cannot be the Kron as the majority of the sales revenue is not denominated in this currency

D   NJ should adopt the Kron as its functional currency

E   NJ must adopt the Kron as its presentational currency

SUBJECT F2: ADVANCED FINANCIAL REPORTING

INTEGRATED REPORTING

155 Complete the sentence below by placing one of the following options in each of the spaces.

| A management commentary | external | value |
| An integrated report | internal | cash |

An integrated report is a concise communication about how an organisation's strategy, governance, performance and prospects, in the context of its *external* environment, lead to the creation of *value* over the short, medium and long term.

156 Which of the following are categories of 'the capitals' in the International <IR> Framework? Select all that apply:

- A Embedded
- B Social and relationship ✓
- C Financial ✓
- D Intellectual ✓
- E Human ✓
- F Manufactured ✓
- G Real

157 Which THREE of the following statements relating to the International <IR> Framework are correct?

- (A) It takes a principles-based approach
- B An integrated report must be a standalone report ✗
- (C) It does not prescribe specific key performance indicators ✗
- D It provides guidance only, as it does not include any specific requirements that must be applied → It has some compulsory element to comply.
- E An integrated report must adopt the categorisation of the capitals in the <IR> Framework — is not required.
- (F) It can also be applied, adapted as necessary, by public sector and not-for-profit organizations

158 Which one of the following could be construed as a benefit of <IR>?

- A <IR> removes the focus of an entity's reporting away from traditional financial values and benefits
- B Competitors obtain improved levels of understanding regarding the entity ✗
- C Increased preparatory time and costs ✗
- D The use of a principles-based rather than a rules-based approach to <IR> increases the levels of subjectivity and judgement within the <IR> ✗

159 L'Hotel Emilia is a hotel and spa with a large estate that can be used by guests. Within its private estate is a natural fresh water lake and waterfall that can be used for fishing, aquatic sports and is used as a source for hydro-electric power by the hotel.

In the integrated report of L'Hotel Emilia, which of the following capitals would be the most appropriate under which to disclose these details?

- A Financial
- B Intellectual
- C Natural *(selected)*
- D Environmental

ANALYSING FINANCIAL STATEMENTS

160 The following is an extract from the statement of financial position of KER:

	$ million
Equity:	
Share capital ($1 shares)	100
Revaluation surplus	74
Other reserves	32
Retained earnings	457
Total equity	663
Non-current liabilities	
Long-term borrowings	400 → Debt
Redeemable preference shares	100 → Debt
Deferred tax	37
Warranty provision	12
Total non-current liabilities	549

Giving your answer as a percentage to one decimal place, what is KER's gearing ratio (calculated as debt/equity)?

Gearing ratio = Debt / Equity → (400 + 100) / 663 = 75.4%

SUBJECT F2: ADVANCED FINANCIAL REPORTING

161 Extracts from the statement of profit or loss of GD for the year ended 30 June 20X1:

	$m
Gross profit	360
Distribution costs	(40)
Administrative expenses	(130)
Finance costs	(11)
Profit before tax	179

Extracts from the statement of financial position of GD as at 30 June 20X1

	$m
Non-current liabilities:	
Long-term borrowings	90
Deferred taxation	15
	105

Calculate the <u>interest cover</u> for GD for the year to 30 June 20X1.

Give your answer to one decimal place.

Interest cover = Operating profit / Finance cost = (179+11)/11 = 17.3

162 Extracts from the statement of profit or loss of SDF for the year ended 31 October 20X1

	$m
Gross profit	268
Operating expenses	(55)
Share of profit of associate	37
Finance costs	(12)
Profit before tax	238

Operating profit 268 − 55 = ... = 37.4%
Capital employed 465 + 190 − 86

Extracts from the statement of financial position of SDF as at 31 October 20X1

	$m
Non-current assets:	
Property, plant and equipment	381
Investment in associate	86 —
	467
Equity:	
Share capital	200
Retained reserves	265
Total equity	465 —
Non-current liabilities:	
Long-term borrowings	190 —
Deferred tax	25

Calculate the <u>return on capital employed</u> of SDF for the year to 31 October 20X1, excluding the impact of the associate from your calculation.

Give your answer as a percentage to one decimal place.

163 The Return on Capital Employed (ROCE) for DF has increased from 12.3% to 17.8% in the year to 31 March 20X5.

Which one of the following independent options would be a valid reason for this increase?

- A Significant investment in property, plant and equipment shortly before the year end
- B Revaluation of land and buildings following a change of policy from cost model to revaluation model
- C Property, plant and equipment acquired in the previous period now operating at full capacity
- D An issue of equity shares with the proceeds being used to repay long-term borrowings

164 The following is an extract from the financial statements of ST for the year to 31 December 20X3:

Equity and liabilities	20X3 $m	20X2 $m
Share capital	400	250
Share premium	200	50
Revaluation surplus	158	35
Retained earnings	350	470
Total equity	**1,108**	**805**
Non-current liabilities		
Long-term borrowings	530	480

Which THREE of the following statements about the changes in the capital structure of ST could be realistically concluded from the extract provided above?

- A ST must have made a loss in the year as retained earnings have fallen
- B A revaluation surplus in the year has contributed to the reduction in gearing
- C Shares were issued at a premium to nominal value
- D ST may have paid a significant dividend in the year
- E ST must have secured additional long-term borrowings of $50m

SUBJECT F2: ADVANCED FINANCIAL REPORTING

165 An investor is considering two potential investments, A and B, and extracts from the entities' statements of financial position are below:

	A	B
	$000	$000
Total equity	3,754	3,403
Non-current liabilities:		
5% loan notes	1,000	200
Current liabilities:		
Short-term borrowings	50	80

Entity B's gearing ratio has been calculated to be 5.9%.

The gearing ratio of A that would be comparable with B's ratio above (to the nearest decimal place) is:

A   21.0%

B   21.9%

C   26.6%

D   28.0%

166 LOP operates in the construction industry, is listed on its local stock exchange and prepares its financial statements in accordance with IFRS standards. It is looking to expand overseas by acquiring a new subsidiary. Two geographical areas have been targeted, Frontland and Sideland. Entity A operates in Frontland and entity B operates in Sideland. Both entities are listed on their local exchanges.

The financial highlights for entities A, B and LOP are provided below for the last trading period.

	A	B	LOP
Revenue	$160m	$300m	$500m
Gross profit margin	26%	17%	28%
Profit from operations margin	9%	11%	16%

Which one of the following statements is a realistic conclusion that could be drawn from the above information?

A   A appears to be benefiting from economies of scale

B   B has lower operating expenses than A

C   A's high gross profit margin and low operating profit margin proves that the directors of A are partaking in creative accounting

D   Acquisition of either entity would lead to an improvement in LOP's gross margin due to the increased revenue that would be achieved

167 Klop operates in the construction industry, is listed on its local stock exchange and prepares its financial statements in accordance with IFRS standards. It is looking to expand overseas by acquiring a new subsidiary.

The financial highlights for entities VVD, ROB and Klop are provided below for the last trading period.

	VVD	ROB	Klop
Revenue	$160m	$300m	$500m
Gross profit margin	26%	17%	28%
Profit from operations margin	9%	11%	16%
Gearing	65%	30%	38%
Average rate of interest available in the last 12 months	5%	9%	8%

Which of the following statements is true, based on the information provided?

A   VVD would be a riskier investment than ROB because it has higher gearing

B   VVD would give Klop greater benefit in terms of additional borrowing capacity

C   VVD has attracted a lower rate of interest on its borrowings than ROB because it's gearing level would suggest that it is a lower risk to lenders than ROB

D   VVD's lower profit from operations margin suggests VVD operates in the budget sector of the construction market compared to ROB and Klop

168 POL is looking to acquiring a new subsidiary, entity A or entity B.

Which one of the following statements is false in regard to the use of ratio analysis to make a decision about investing in A or B?

A   A and B may use different accounting standards when preparing their financial statements and this would reduce the comparability of their profit margins

B   A and B may be subject to different tax rates which would reduce the comparability of their profit from operations margins

C   A and B may apply different accounting policies, such as cost model v revaluation model for property, plant and equipment. This would reduce comparability of their gearing ratios

D   Figures could be distorted due to large transactions prior to the year-end

169 RT is seeking expansion by pursuing new markets with its existing product base. The following is an extract from the statement of profit or loss of RT:

	20X9 $m	20X8 $m
Revenue	1,430	1,022
Cost of sales	(1,058)	(705)
Gross profit	372	317
Administrative expenses	(74)	(62)
Distribution costs	(168)	(100)
Profit from operations	130	155

Which one of the following statements could NOT be realistically concluded from the extract provided above?

A   RT may have increased its sales volumes, and, therefore, revenue, by reducing its selling prices

B   RT's distribution costs have increased in line with the increase in revenue and the main reason for the fall in operating profit margin is the increase in administrative expenses, which should remain relatively fixed

C   The significant increase in distribution costs suggests that RT is supplying goods to new customers that are geographically further away

D   RT's increase in revenue has been achieved at the expense of profit margins

170 The following information is available for 2 potential acquisition targets. The entities are situated in the same country and both operate in the same industry.

	A	B
Revenue	$375m	$380m
Gross profit margin	28%	19%
Profit for the year/revenue margin	11%	11%

Which one of the following statements is NOT a valid conclusion that could be drawn from comparing the above information for A and B?

A   A's gross profit margin is better than B's as it is able to benefit from economies of scale

B   The difference between the gross profit margin of A and B may be due to how they classify expenses between cost of sales and operating costs

C   A may have improved its gross profit margin by significant investment in new and efficient machinery, but could be suffering from high finance costs as a result of financing the investment with long-term borrowings

D   B may be selling a significantly higher volume of products than A but at a lower price

171 Your friend, Amelie, is considering acquiring a small shareholding in AD, an entity listed on the stock market, as she believes that the entity has a promising future. However, having performed some limited analysis on the most recent financial statements of AD, she is concerned by some of her findings. Profitability has reduced in the most recent financial period due to a significant increase in administrative expenses. The return on capital employed has fallen, partly due to the increase in expenses but also from a significant investment in property, plant and equipment close to the year end.

The financial statements reviewed by your friend were for the year ended 30 September 20X1. It is now June 20X2.

OBJECTIVE TEST QUESTIONS : SECTION 1

Which THREE of the following options would be considered realistic next steps for your friend to take prior to investing?

A   Request an analysis of administrative expenses from the entity to understand why it has risen significantly → no access to this info

B   Access articles from the financial press and obtain industry ratio averages and compare performance of AD with other entities in the sector ✓

C   Contact the Chief Financial Officer to ask what is being done to improve profitability and whether the increase in administrative expenses is a one-off event ✓ → no access to this info.

D   Review the narrative reports within the financial statements that give details of recent investment to assess if the business is undergoing expansion and likely to bring additional future returns

E   Obtain a copy of any interim financial statements published since the previous year end to assess whether performance of the entity has improved ✓

172   KL operates in the fashion wholesale business and its management team has become increasingly concerned about the liquidity of the entity. The management team have asked for some detailed analysis and you have calculated the following ratios to help you with your assessment:

	30 June 20X3	30 June 20X2
Inventory holding period	128 days	77 days
Receivables collection period	88 days	87 days
Payables payment period	170 days	118 days
Current ratio	1.3:1	2.1:1
Quick ratio	0.7:1	1.4:1

Which one of the following is NOT a valid statement about the ratios shown above?

A   The increase in inventory holding period is a significant concern as there is a high risk of obsolescence in the industry ✓

B   The deterioration in the ratios shown at the 30 June 20X3 year end could simply be a result of a significant purchase of goods being made on credit terms close to the year end ✓

C   KL are attempting to finance its increased inventory holding period by delaying payments to suppliers ✓

D   The significant increase in payables payment period will have caused the cash position to worsen dramatically ✗ this should improve cash position.

173   The following is an extract from the statement of cash flows for QW for the year ended 31 December 20X1:

	$m
Cash flows from operating activities	750
Cash flows from investing activities	(1,130)
Cash flows from financing activities	320
Net cash flow for the year	(60)
Cash and cash equivalents at start of year	650
Cash and cash equivalents at end of year	590

SUBJECT F2: ADVANCED FINANCIAL REPORTING

Based on the information provided, which one of the following independent statements would be a <u>reasonable conclusion</u> about the financial adaptability of QW for the year to 31 December 20X1?

A   QW is in decline as there is a significant cash outflow in investing activities *means growth.*

(B)   QW has financed a high proportion of its investing activities by utilising its operating cash

C   QW must have made a profit in the year, as it has a net cash inflow from operating activities *It could have significant non-cash items in expense that added back is +.*

D   QW must be facing serious liquidity problems as its cash and cash equivalents have fallen by $60 million throughout the year *& still have positive cash balance.*

174 The following is an extract from the financial statements of EE for the year to 31 December 20X1:

Equity and liabilities	20X1 $m	20X0 $m
Share capital	325	195
Share premium	442	364
Revaluation surplus	455	293
Retained earnings	371	585
Total equity	**1,593**	**1,437**
Non-current liabilities		
Long-term borrowings	585	553

Gearing
X1 37%
X0 38%

Which of the following statements about the <u>changes in the capital structure of EE</u> is a <u>valid conclusion</u> when reviewing the extract provided above?

A   EE must have made a loss in the year as retained earnings have fallen *or could paid dividend*

B   A revaluation surplus in the year has contributed to a <u>reduction in gearing</u>

C   Bonus issues were the only share issues during the year and caused the increase in share capital ✗

D   EE must have secured additional long-term borrowings of $25m ✗

175 BH is analysing the financial statements of two potential acquisition targets, VB and JK. VB and JK are of a similar size and operate in the same industry. The <u>gearing</u> of each entity is as follows:

	VB	JK
Gearing	54.3%	31.7%

Debt / Equity.

Which <u>TWO</u> of the following statements could realistically explain the significant difference between the two entities' gearing ratio shown above?

A   VB has recorded significant gains on the change in fair value of its FVOCI investments

B   VB's management is better at controlling costs than JK's ✗

C   VB uses the cost model for property, plant and equipment whereas JK uses the revaluation model

D   VB has reduced its effective tax rate by employing tax accountants ✗

E   VB relies more on debt finance, whereas JK relies on equity finance

OBJECTIVE TEST QUESTIONS : SECTION 1

176 ABC is a small private entity looking for investment. It has been trading for more than 10 years, manufacturing and selling its own branded perfumes, lotions and candles to the public in its 15 retail stores and to other larger retailing entities. Revenue and profits have been steady over the last 10 years, however, about 15 months ago, ABC set up an online shop and also secured a lucrative deal with a boutique hotel chain to supply products carrying the hotel name and logo.

Extracts from the statement of profit or loss of ABC are provided below:

	20X2 $000	20X1 $000
Revenue	6,000	3,700
Gross profit	1,917	1,095
Profit before tax	540	307

The revenue and profits of the three business segments for the year ended 31 December 20X2 were:

	Retail operations $000	Online store $000	Hotel contract $000
Revenue	4,004	1,096	900
Gross profit	1,200	330	387
Profit before tax	320	138	82

The online store and hotel contract earned a negligible amount of revenue and profit in the year ended 31 December 20X1.

Which THREE of the following statements about the performance of ABC in the year ended 31 December 20X2 could be realistically concluded from the extracts provided above?

A The revenue growth is principally due to the online store and hotel contract

B The gross profit margin would have fallen in 20X2 if the new operations had not been introduced

C The online store should have a better gross profit margin than retail operations as it does not have the shop overheads

D The hotel contract attracts a higher gross profit margin than the other operations

E The hotel contract appears to require significant overheads in comparison to revenue when compared with the other segments

F The increase in profit before tax margin is principally due to the hotel contract

177 CB had 3,750,000 $1 ordinary shares in issue at 1 February 20X4 and did not issue any new shares throughout the year ended 31 January 20X5. It reported a profit for the year ended 31 January 20X5 of $750,000. Dividends of 50c per share were paid during the year.

Calculate the dividend cover for CB at 31 January 20X5.

Give your answer to two decimal places.

178 RT is analysing the financial statements of two potential acquisition targets, X and Y, which are of a similar size. The non-current asset turnovers of the two entities are as follows:

	A	B
Non-current asset turnover	3.6	1.1

SUBJECT F2: ADVANCED FINANCIAL REPORTING

Which THREE of the following statements could realistically explain the significant difference between the two entities' non-current asset turnover shown above?

- A   A's non-current assets are operating more efficiently than B's
- B   B has invested in new non-current assets close to the year end
- C   A has revalued its non-current assets during the year
- D   A operates in a manufacturing industry and B in a service industry
- E   A's non-current assets are significantly older than B's

179 Place the following options into the highlighted boxes in the table below to correctly reflect the formulae used to calculate dividend cover.

| Net profit for the year |
| Share price |
| Dividend per share |
| Dividend paid during the year |
| Number of ordinary shares issued |

| Dividend cover |
| Net profit for the year |
| ─────────────── |
| Dividend paid during the y- |

180 SJ bought an item of plant and machinery for $150,000 on 31 March 20X6, and financed the purchase by taking out a bank loan. The year end is 31 March 20X6.

Which of the following statements are false?

- A   SJ's current ratio would remain unaffected by the transaction
- B   SJ's gearing would increase due to the increase in debt as at the year end.
- C   Interest cover would decrease due to the increased finance costs incurred during the year ended 31 Mar 20X6.
- D   ROCE would be expected to reduce as operating profits would be unaffected and capital employed would increase

Op profit / Finance cost

181 XZ has changed its accounting policy in the year and now revalues all of its non-depreciable land.   → Equity + NCA.

Which THREE of the following ratios would be directly affected by this change in policy resulting in a lack of comparability between this year's ratio and that calculated last year?

- A   Non-current asset turnover   Revenue/NCA
- B   Profit before tax margin   Profit/Revenue
- C   Return on capital employed   Op profit/capital employed (Equity + debt − Inv. associated)
- D   Gearing   Debt/Equity
- E   Current ratio   CA/CL

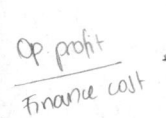

OBJECTIVE TEST QUESTIONS : SECTION 1

182 The directors of EMS have recently submitted a loan application for $100 million to finance expansion and have attached EMS's most recent financial statements in support of the application.

Financial highlights from the financial statements are as follows:

	20X2	20X1
Gross profit margin	27.7%	25.5%
Profit before tax margin	12.8%	9.2%
Return on capital employed	15.5%	16.1%

Extracts from the statement of financial position as at 31 December:

	20X2	20X1
Equity		
Share capital	400	400
Revaluation surplus	555	180
Other reserves	154	154
Retained earnings	911	743
Total equity	2,020	1,477
Borrowings		
Long-term – 5% convertible bonds 20X4	300	288
Short-term	68	–
	368	288

Which one of the following statements provides a valid and reasonable explanation for the reduction in return on capital employed?

A Additional long-term borrowings taken out

B Increased finance cost from short-term borrowings

C Reduction in profit from operations margin

D Revaluation of property, plant and equipment

183 Extracts from the financial statements of JPS are shown below

Extracts from the statement of financial position

	20X2	20X1
Assets	$m	$m
Property, plant and equipment	1,532	896
Cash and cash equivalents	–	288
Equity		
Share capital	600	600
Revaluation surplus	310	140
Other reserves	88	88
Retained earnings	1,602	1,266
Total equity	2,600	2,094

61

Borrowings

Long-term – 5% convertible bonds 20X4	400	376
Short-term	116	

Extracts from statement of profit or loss

Revenue	4,800	4,040

Calculate the asset turnover (based on capital employed) for the year ended 31 December 20X2, including both long-term and short-term borrowings. State your answer to two decimal places.

$$\frac{4,800}{400 + 116 + 2600} = 1.54$$

184 A professional accountant is reviewing the financial statements of EMS on behalf of one of EMS's shareholders.

Financial highlights from the financial statements are as follows:

	20X2	20X1
Revenue	$2,400m	$2,020m
Profit before tax margin	12.8%	9.2%

Extracts from statement of financial position as at 31 December:

	20X2	20X1
Assets	$m	$m
Property, plant and equipment	766	448
Equity		
Share capital	300	300
Revaluation surplus	155	70
Other reserves	44	44
Retained earnings	801	633
Total equity	1,300	1,047

Which one of the following is an inappropriate statement regarding the limitations of using the above financial information when making a decision about whether to provide finance to EMS?

A Different accounting policies can affect comparison of one period to the next x

B Limited extracts are provided from the statement of financial position so the analysts are unable to assess how well EMS manages its working capital x

C Limited extracts are provided from the statement of profit or loss so the analysts are unable to see the reason for the improvement in profit before tax margin ✓

D No industry averages are available so the analysts cannot see whether improvement is in line with, or exceeds, expectations

OBJECTIVE TEST QUESTIONS : SECTION 1

185 Extract from the statements of profit or loss of A and B for the year ended 31 December 20X1

	A	B
	$000	$000
Gross profit	1,100	1,580
Distribution costs	(375)	(420)
Administrative expenses	(168)	(644)
Share of associate profit	148	25
Finance costs	(25)	(32)
Profit before tax	680	509

Extract from the statements of financial position of A and B as at 31 December 20X1

	$000	$000
Investment in associate	570	350
Total equity	950	1,500
Non-current liabilities (borrowings)	500	650

The return on capital employed of B has been calculated as 28.7%.

The return on capital employed of A that would be comparable to B's on a like for like basis is:

- A 38.4%
- B 46.9%
- C 48.6%
- D 63.3%

186 Complete the following sentences by placing one of the options identified below in each of the spaces. The options may be used more than once.

| an increase | a reduction |

When assessing reasons for changes in cash and cash equivalents _____ in inventory, _____ in receivables and _____ in payables would all explain an improvement in the cash position.

187 RB is considering investing in LW, a listed entity that operates in the manufacturing sector. LW operates in a mature market and has not experienced growth in volume for the past five years. It is currently considering methods of increasing revenue by diversifying its product range, however it has yet to implement any new strategy.

The following ratios have been calculated based on LW's most recent financial statements for the year ended 31 December 20X3.

	20X3	20X2
Gross profit margin	39.4%	36.6%
Operating profit margin	12.6%	14.4%
Quick ratio	0.5	1.1
Inventories holding period	141 days	112 days
Payables payment period	154 days	98 days

SUBJECT F2: ADVANCED FINANCIAL REPORTING

LW was involved in a major dispute with one of its key customers in 20X3 regarding the non-settlement of amounts owed by the customer. The dispute was eventually settled close to the reporting date and the majority of the cash has since been received, however LW incurred significant legal fees in the process and had to stop supplying the customer for a period of time.

Which THREE of the following statements are realistic conclusions that could be drawn from the above ratios and information?

- **A** Stopping supplies to the significant customer will have contributed to the increase in inventory holding period
- **B** The impact of the cost of the dispute can be seen in the operating profit margin, which has fallen despite an increase in gross profit margin for the year
- C The increase in gross profit margin is likely to have been achieved by increasing selling prices → unlikely to increase selling price with no growth
- D The increase in payables payment period will have resulted in a reduction in cash and cash equivalents ✗   improve
- E The reduction in quick ratio is principally due to the significant increase in inventory holding period ✗
- **F** The reduction in quick ratio is principally due to the significant increase in payables payment period

188 BR is looking to invest in a company, WL. Which of the following would NOT be readily available to help BR decide whether to invest in WL?

Select ALL that apply.

- **A** Breakdown of operating expenses to establish reasons for fall in operating margin ✗
- **B** Cash flow forecasts to assess likely post year end liquidity
- C Industry average statistics to compare performance with other entities in the sector ✓
- ~~D~~ Interim financial information that may have been published since the 20X3 year end
   ↳ typically published by listed entities
- E Operating and financial review (management commentary) ✓

189 Place the following options into the highlighted boxes in the table below to correctly reflect the formulae used to calculate both return on capital employed and gross profit margin. The same option may be used more than once.

Revenue
Revenue – cost of sales
Equity
Revenue – cost of sales – operating expenses
Non-current assets
~~Capital employed~~

Return on capital employed	Gross profit margin
Revenue – cost of sale – op exp / Capital employed	Revenue – cost of sales / Revenue

190 Which one of the following statements is NOT a limitation of comparing ratios of two entities listed on stock exchanges in different countries?

A   If entities are located in different geographical markets, they may be exposed to different economic pressures and variables such as interest rates and tax rates which will distort any comparison of earnings per share

B   The dividend cover will be incomparable as share prices may be affected by differing levels of liquidity in their respective markets

C   The financial statements of the entities could be prepared using different accounting standards, resulting in incomparable earnings per share

D   The companies can use different calculations to determine the same ratio.

191 Which of the following would be readily available information to a minority shareholder of a listed entity?

Select ALL that apply.

A   Cash flow forecasts for the next five years

B   Share price information

C   Operating and financial review/management commentary

D   Trend analysis (published results over a period of time)

E   Analysis of expenses

F   Size of order book (to assess future prospects)

192 ABC prepares its financial statements in accordance with International Financial Reporting Standards and is listed on its local stock exchange. ABC is considering the acquisition of overseas operations. Two geographical areas have been targeted, X-land and Y-land. Entity X operates in X-land and entity Y operates in Y-land.

The most recent financial statements of entities X and Y have been converted into ABC's currency for ease of comparison. The financial indicators from these financial statements are provided below.

	X	Y
Revenue	$390m	$400m
Gross profit margin	28%	19%
Profit after tax/revenue × 100	10%	11%

Which one of the following statements is NOT a valid potential explanation of the difference in gross profit margins reflected above?

A   X and Y do not operate in the same industry

B   X and Y sell the same products but have a different sales/product mix

C   X classifies certain expenses as cost of sales that Y classifies as operating expenses

D   X sells lower volume but higher quality products than Y

65

SUBJECT F2: ADVANCED FINANCIAL REPORTING

193 Ratios based upon the most recent financial statements of entities A and B are provided below.

	A	B
Gearing Debt/Equity	66%	26%
Average rate of interest available in the respective markets	5%	10%

Which one of the following statements would NOT be a valid explanation of the difference in gearing ratios reflected above?

- A A has recently replaced its plant and equipment and B is yet to do so ✓
- B A revalues its non-current assets whereas B uses the cost model
- C A wishes to limit its voting rights to a small number of shareholders
- D A wishes to take advantage of relatively cheap debt finance ✓

194 ABC prepares its financial statements in accordance with International Financial Reporting Standards and is listed on its local stock exchange. ABC is considering the acquisition of one of two potential targets, X and Y.

ABC's mergers and acquisitions department has calculated gearing for each entity as:

	X	Y
Gearing Debt/Equity	74%	18%

Complete the following sentences by placing one of the options identified below in each of the spaces.

X	Y	ABC
less	more	

If further debt finance was required by the new companies, debt finance would be _more_ likely to be obtained for Y.

Based upon the gearing levels of the two entities, an investment in __X__ would appear to be riskier than an investment in __Y__.

195 The following information is available for entity SAF:

Six month period ended:	31 Dec 20X2	30 Jun 20X2
Revenue	$3.1m	$2m
Gross profit margin	21.9%	27.5%
Current ratio	2.0	2.4
Quick ratio	1.2	1.6
Inventories holding period	92 days	58 days
Receivables collection period	101 days	72 days
Payables payment period	90 days	73 days

Which TWO of the following statements about SAF could NOT be realistically concluded from the above financial information?

- A SAF is facing serious liquidity problems
- B The increase in inventories holding period may be in response to the extra demand for products reflected in the increased revenue
- C The reduction in quick ratio is caused by the increase in inventory holding period
- D The significant expansion in revenue is likely to have been achieved by reducing selling prices
- E There are signs of over-trading

196 **Which one of the following statements correctly identifies the effect that an upwards revaluation of non-current assets would have on return on capital employed (ROCE) and gearing?**

- A Increase in both ROCE and gearing
- B Decrease in both ROCE and gearing
- C Increase in ROCE and decrease in gearing
- D Decrease in ROCE and increase in gearing

197 **Which of the following would be accessible information for a potential lender of a significant level of finance?**

Select ALL that apply.

- A Cash flow forecasts for the next five years
- B Information about existing finance arrangements
- C Operating and financial review/management commentary
- D Trend analysis (published results over a period of time)
- E Detailed analysis of expenses
- F Size of order book (to assess future prospects)

198 XZ is seeking to grow through acquisition and has identified two unlisted entities as potential acquisition targets, A and B. A and B are of a similar size and operate in the same line of business and in the same country. A and B have similar levels of capital employed, but the balance between equity and debt differs.

Extracts from the most recent financial statements are:

Statement of profit or loss and other comprehensive income	A	B
	$000	$000
Revenue	5,700	5,300
Other comprehensive income:		
Revaluation surplus	200	–

SUBJECT F2: ADVANCED FINANCIAL REPORTING

The following key financial ratios have been calculated to assist with the investment decision.

	A	B
Gross profit margin	36.0%	31.0%
Profit before interest and tax margin	11.5%	14.0%
Return on capital employed	27.4%	22.2%

Complete the following sentences by placing one of the options identified below in each of the spaces.

higher	because of
lower	despite

A is incurring significantly ___higher___ operating expenses than B. Its return on capital employed is higher than B's ___despite___ the revaluation of non-current assets in the year.

199 XZ is seeking to grow through acquisition and has identified two unlisted entities as potential acquisition targets, A and B. A and B are of similar size and operate in the same line of business and in the same country. A and B have similar levels of capital employed, but the balance between equity and debt differs.

Extracts from the most recent financial statements are:

Statement of profit or loss and other comprehensive income	A	B
	$000	$000
Finance costs	(120)	(105)
Other comprehensive income:		
Revaluation surplus	200	–

The following key financial ratios have been calculated to assist with the investment decision.

	A	B
Gearing (at the year-end)	34.3%	55.2%

Which one of the following statements would NOT be a valid explanation for the difference in gearing and finance costs between A and B?

A   A has a revaluation policy for its non-current assets whereas B adopts the cost model

B   B distributes more of its profits to its shareholders in dividend payments

C   A pays a higher rate of interest on its borrowings

D   If the rate of interest on borrowings is similar for both entities, then either A has increased its borrowings or B has repaid a significant amount of borrowings part way through the year

OBJECTIVE TEST QUESTIONS : SECTION 1

200 A Ltd has purchased its computer equipment using long term debt finance, whereas B Ltd leases computer equipment under a lease agreement. The leases were deemed low value leases and, therefore, B elects to use the exemption from recording a lease liability. Both entities use their computer equipment for administrative purposes.

Which of the following ratios would be considered incomparable between the two entities based on the way the entities have financed their purchases of computer equipment?

Select ALL that apply.

- A Gross profit margin ✓
- B Non-current asset turnover ✓
- C Return on capital employed
- D Current ratio ✓
- E Gearing
- F Interest cover

The ratios which use finance costs and debt are deemed distorted for direct comparison.

201 The following is an extract from the financial statements of WX for the year to 31 December 20X5:

Equity and liabilities	20X5 $m	20X4 $m
Share capital	500	400
Share premium	300	400
Revaluation surplus	340	–
Retained earnings	300	470
Total equity	**1,440**	**1,270**
Non-current liabilities		
Long-term borrowings	360	320

seems like a bonus issue.

Which one of the following statements about the changes in the capital structure of WX is a valid conclusion that can be drawn from the extract provided above?

- A WX must have made a loss in the year, *could also be due to dividend payment.*
- B WX may have adopted the revaluation policy to offset a significant loss in the year and maintain the gearing level ✓
- C WX has raised finance via a share issue
- D WX must have taken out additional borrowings of $40 million ✗

SUBJECT F2: ADVANCED FINANCIAL REPORTING

202 Complete the following sentences by placing one of the options identified below in each of the spaces. The options may be used more than once.

| operating | investing | financing |

When analysing a statement of cash flows, a cash outflow from _investing_ activities would suggest that the entity is expanding its operations.

An outflow from investing activities is often matched with an inflow from _financing_ activities as long term finance should be used to finance investment.

203 TYU is a listed entity that operates in a highly competitive market. A new entrant to this market has created pressure amongst the competitive entities by developing a marginally lower quality product and selling it at a lower price. The result has been a shift in market share to this new entrant in the last few months of the financial period just ended.

Extracts from TYU's financial information for the year are as follows:

	20X2	20X1
	$	$
Revenue	$678m	$618m
Gross profit margin	32.4%	35.0%

Complete the following sentences by placing one of the options identified below in each of the spaces.

| a reduction in selling prices | an increase in cost of sales per unit |

Given the circumstances that TYU finds itself in, the most likely reason for the reduction in gross profit margin is _a reduction in selling prices_.

204 Extracts from BRO's financial information for the year are as follows:

	20X2	20X1
	$	$
Revenue	$678m	$618m
Gross profit margin	32.4%	35.0%
Current ratio CA/CL	1.3	2.0
Quick ratio CA-Inv/CL	0.5	1.1
Inventories holding period Inv/Cost of sales × 365	167 days	100 days
Cash and cash equivalents	–	$24m

Which one of the following statements is a valid conclusion that can be drawn from the above ratios?

A   The increase in inventory holding period has resulted in a fall in current ratio ✗

B   The increase in inventory holding period has resulted in a fall in quick ratio ✗

C   The increase in the inventory holding period has resulted in a reduction in cash

D   The increase in inventory holding period has resulted in a fall in gross profit margin

205 UYT is a listed entity that operates in a highly competitive market.

Extracts from UYT's financial information for the year are as follows:

	20X2	20X1
	$	$
Revenue	$678m	$618m
Gross profit margin	32.4%	35.0%
Operating profit margin	5.2%	4.6%
Current ratio	1.3	2.0
Quick ratio	0.5	1.1
Receivables collection period	65 days	60 days
Payables payment period	156 days	109 days
Cash and cash equivalents	–	$24m

Which one of the following statements is NOT a valid conclusion that can be drawn from the above ratios?

A As the current ratio is greater than 1 there are no major liquidity concerns ✓ Quick ratio only 0.5

B The increase in payables payment period has been caused by the lack of cash

C The increase in receivables collection period has contributed to the lack of cash ✓

D The management of UYT have controlled costs well to minimise the impact of the competitive environment

206 Which of the following differences in accounting policies between two entities could affect the comparison of their gross profit margins?

Select ALL that apply.

A Different depreciation rates on plant and equipment

B First-in-first-out versus average cost method for valuing inventory

C The method for valuing non-controlling interest at the date of acquisition of a subsidiary → only affect the calculation of goodwill and the nci share of equity

D Revaluation of non-current assets versus cost model

E Different classification of costs between cost of sales and operating expenses

F Input (cost) basis versus output (work certified) basis for calculating stage of completion of a contract with a customer which recognises revenue over time

207 Below are extracts from the statement of profit or loss and other comprehensive income of JS Inc for the year ended 31 October 20X5:

	$000
Gross profit	430
Distribution costs	(32)
Administrative expenses	(159)
Operating profit	239
Finance costs	(15)
Profit before tax	224

SUBJECT F2: ADVANCED FINANCIAL REPORTING

Included within administrative expenses was $15,000 of depreciation, $23,000 salaries to staff and $12,000 amortisation of intangible assets.

Included within distribution expenses are $5,000 of depreciation and $8,000 fuel costs.

EBITDA for JS Inc for the year ended 31 October 20X5 is (quoted in $000's):

   A   146
   B   177
   C   271
   D   302

208 The Gartner Data Analytics Maturity model consists of 4 stages. Which of the following is one of these stages?

   A   Qualitative
   B   Logistic
   C   Prescriptive
   D   Interrogative

RANDOM QUESTION TESTS

RANDOM QUESTION TEST 1

1.1 Stark Co is an innovative technology company producing high specification robotic equipment. The finance director is considering the accounting treatment of two potential intangible assets, as follows:

- Stark Co recently acquired a 20-year patent for the 'Future-suture', a new product invented internally by Stark Co that can be used during complicated medical procedures

- a list of customer contacts which has grown over the years at a similar rate to the growth of the Stark Co business.

What would be the correct accounting treatment of these intangible assets as per IAS 38 *Intangible assets*?

	Patent	Customer list
A	Not recorded	Not recorded
B	Capitalised and amortised over 20 years	Capitalised and amortised over expected lifetime
C	Capitalised and amortised over 20 years	Not recorded
D	Not recorded	Capitalised and amortised over expected lifetime

OBJECTIVE TEST QUESTIONS : SECTION 1

1.2 AB issued 30,000 5% $100 bonds on 1 January 20X1 at par value, incurring issue costs of $25,000. The bonds will be redeemed after five years at a premium of 10%. Which one of the following statements is correct?

- A The bonds are classified as an amortised cost financial asset
- B The effective rate of interest on the bonds is greater than 5%
- C The initial recognition of the bonds will be at a value of $3,025,000
- D The carrying amount of the bond at each year end will always be $3,300,000

1.3 PF Ltd has issued irredeemable 12% bonds with a market value of $91. The cost of debt is 9.76%.

What is the tax rate used in PF's jurisdiction to the nearest %?

1.4 TUS has an 80% subsidiary, WXV. WXV, which has been a subsidiary of TUS for the whole year, reported a profit after tax of $600,000 in its own financial statements. You ascertain the following additional matters:

At the year-end, there is an unrealised profit of $60,000 on sales by WXV to TUS.

During the year, the goodwill on acquisition of WXV was impaired by $50,000.

TUS measures the non-controlling interest in WXV using the fair value method.

What is the non-controlling interest in WXV that would be reported in the consolidated statement of profit or loss and other comprehensive income of TUS for the year?

- A $98,000
- B $108,000
- C $110,000
- D $120,000

1.5 The following extracts of the financial statements of Couts Ltd have been obtained:

	20X5
Inventories	$195,000
Receivables	$120,000
Cash	$15,000
Loan repayable 20X8	$135,000
Deferred tax	$21,000
Payables	$105,000
Overdraft	$51,000

What is the quick ratio of Couts Ltd?

- A 0.76:1
- B 0.87:1
- C 1.86:1
- D 2.12:1

73

SUBJECT F2: ADVANCED FINANCIAL REPORTING

1.6 Which of the following is **not a valid reason** for an **increase in the level of gearing**?

- A   A revaluation loss has been recorded in the year ✓
- B   New shares were issued during the year
- C   A new loan has been taken out in the year
- D   New high value assets were acquired financed by issuing bonds during the year

↑ Debt
↓ Equity

1.7 EMI owns 75% of the 1m ordinary shares of LI. EMI's holding in LI was acquired on 31 July 20X9 with a cost of $10m to be paid in cash in 1 year's time. EMI's year-end is 31 December 20X9. Goodwill is calculated using the fair value method. just 6 month.

Which of the following statements are correct? Select all that apply.

- A   The non-controlling interest as at the year-end would include a share of any impairment of LI's goodwill.
- B   The goodwill of LI will include the fair value of the net assets of LI as at the 31 December 20X8. ✗
- C   The cost of the investment included within the goodwill calculation is $10m. ✗ VP≠10m.
- D   EMI group retained earnings will include 75% of LI's post-acquisition profits.
- E   The group's consolidated statement of profit or loss will include 100% of LI's income and expenses for the year ended 31 December 20X9. no just 6 months.

1.8 BET is a construction company. BET have entered into a contract with HPY to build a large theme park on land owned by HPY. The job was expected to take 4 years to complete. The contract price was agreed at $12m. The contract was expected to make a profit.

BET uses the work certified basis to determine the stage of completion. By the end of the 2nd year, a surveyor considered the contract to be 65% complete. $3.25m revenue was recorded during year 1.

What amount of revenue will be recorded within the statement of profit or loss for year 2?

- A $3.25m
- B $4.55m
- C $7.80m
- D $12m

12 → 65% → 7.80 → 1y 3.25
        → 2y 4.55

OBJECTIVE TEST QUESTIONS : SECTION 1

1.9 SHA owns 70% of RAT. SHA regularly purchases goods from RAT. On the 28 November 20X1, RAT despatched goods with a selling value of $2.5m to SHA. The goods were not delivered to SHA until 5 December 20X1. At the year-ended 30 November 20X1, SHA's statement of financial position showed a trade payable owed to RAT of $45m.

What is the impact of the adjustment caused by the intra-group trading within the consolidated statement of financial position of the SHA group?

   A Inventory increases by $2.5m
      Receivables decreases by $45m
      Payables decreases by $45m

   B Inventory decreases by $2.5m
      Receivables decreases by $45m
      Payables decreases by 45m

   C Inventory increases by $2.5m
      Receivables decreases by $45m
      Payables decreases by $47.5m

   D Inventory increases by $2.5m
      Receivables decreases by $47.5m
      Payables decreases by $45m

1.10 Y and Z operate in a similar industry. Y has payables days of 35 days. Z has payables days of 88 days. Both entities buy goods on 60-day payment terms and offer customers 30-day payment terms. No settlement discounts are available to or offered by the entities.

Which of the following statements are reasonable? Choose all that apply.

   A Analysis should be made of Z's liquidity to assess whether its long payable days indicate cash flow problems.

   B Company Y is operating efficiently and managing their cash balances as effectively as possible by paying suppliers on time.

   C Both companies have negotiated well with suppliers to obtain credit terms which are longer than the credit terms the companies offer to their customers.

   D Company Z's directors are displaying good management by retaining cash for longer as it is a cheap source of finance.

   E Company Y requires an overdraft to finance its business model.

   F Company Z is at risk of stock outs if suppliers refuse to continue to sell on credit.

RANDOM QUESTION TEST 2

2.1 Suarez Ltd's financial statements for the year ended 31 December 20X5 include a provision of $1m in relation to a court case. Suarez is being sued as an employee was injured as a result of an 'incident' involving the chief executive after an important client tender had been lost. The court case has been contested for a long period of time and the carrying amount of the provision at 31 December 20X4 was $500,000.

The provision will not be considered for tax purposes until any damages are paid. The tax rate in the jurisdiction in which Suarez Ltd is operational is 25%.

SUBJECT F2: ADVANCED FINANCIAL REPORTING

Which one of the following statements is true?

A   The deferred tax liability as at the year-end will have a value of $250,000

B   A charge to reserves of $125,000 will be recorded during the year ended 31 December 20X5

C   A debit to the deferred tax balance on the statement of financial position is required

D   The temporary difference between the carrying amount and the tax base as at the year ended 31 December 20X5 is $500,000

2.2 Which ONE of the following statements is a characteristic of ordinary shares?

A   The dividend payment is a fixed proportion of the nominal value of the shares

B   Upon liquidation of a company, the shareholders will receive a pay-out after all other finance providers have been paid

C   Dividends are treated as a finance cost and are paid out of pre-tax profits

D   The shareholders do not have any right to vote on key matters

2.3 Gerrard's financial statements for the year ended 31 December 20X5 show a profit for the year of $3.4million. On 1 January, Gerrard had 4 million shares in issue. On 1 April, 1 million new shares were issued at the full market price.

Gerrard also have $2.5 million 5% convertible loan stock in issue, which can be converted this year into 40 shares for every $100. Gerrard pays tax at 26%. The carrying amount of the liability element of the convertible loan stock is $2million. The effective interest rate is 8%.

What are Gerrard's basic and diluted earnings per share for the year ended 31 December 20X5?

	Basic earnings per share	Diluted earnings per share
A	71.6 cents	61.2 cents
B	71.6 cents	60.7 cents
C	68 cents	58.2 cents
D	68 cents	58.6 cents

2.4 Which of the following items is unlikely to be considered a 'one-off' item which would impact the comparability of ratios?

A   A new website selling direct to the public has meant that deliveries are now made to more diverse geographical areas, increasing delivery costs

B   A closure of a department has led to redundancies

C   Sale of surplus property leading to a profit on disposal

D   A storm in the year led to significant damage to the warehouse

OBJECTIVE TEST QUESTIONS : SECTION 1

2.5 SJ purchased 20% of the ordinary shares of JB on 1 January 20X4 for $937,500. SJ acquired 100% of the ordinary share capital of DP on 1 January 20X5 for $4,650,000. These are the only investments in equity shares owned by SJ. SJ calculates non-controlling interest using the proportionate method. SJ is deemed to have significant influence upon JB.

Which one of the following statements is correct?

- A   SJ Group prepares consolidated financial statements from 1 January 20X4
- B   The cost of investment used within the investment in associate calculation is $937,500
- C   No non-controlling interest is shown in SJ Group's statement of financial position
- D   The assets and liabilities of SJ, DP and JB will be 100% consolidated within the SJ Group statement of financial position

2.6 Bellamy Ltd is a large supermarket, operating in the UK. Bellamy receives payments from suppliers in return for advantageous shelf positioning and offering the suppliers' goods under promotional prices. Most of these suppliers sign 12 month contracts where payment is made up front. Bellamy has a policy of recognising the revenue from the supplier payments immediately. The Financial Controller for Bellamy thinks that the recognition policy of the payments does not comply with IFRS 15. The Financial Controller approached the Finance Director with these views but was told 'This is how we have always recognised these payments. They don't form part of our main operating income from selling goods so it will not really matter. IFRS 15 is not relevant here.'

Which of the following statements are correct regarding the above scenario? Pick all that apply.

- A   No ethical issues exist as the Finance Director is correct. IFRS 15 is not relevant.
- B   The Financial Controller has a responsibility to follow the orders of the Finance Director and, therefore, no further action should be taken by the Financial Controller.
- C   Revenue should be recognised from the contract as the risks and rewards associated with the goods sold to the supplier are transferred.
- D   Revenue should be recognised to reflect the stage of completion of the contract and when the services are provided to the supplier.
- E   There is an ethical risk that the Finance Director is deliberately overstating revenue. The Financial controller should contact the CIMA ethics helpline.

2.7 The following information in relation to Jolly has been obtained:

	20X8
Revenue	$975,000
Dividends received	$90,000
Dividends paid	$37,500
Cost of sales	$555,000
Finance costs	$45,000
Interest received	$31,500
Operating expenses	$300,000

SUBJECT F2: ADVANCED FINANCIAL REPORTING

What is the operating margin of Jolly?

A   8.5%

B   12.3%

C   17.9%

D   19.7%

2.8 The investors of JS require a return of 8% on their investment. The profits earned by the entity for the year ended 31 December 20X7 were $1.8m. The dividends for 20X7 were recently paid to the owners of JS's 1m ordinary shares. The dividend payment totalled $600,000. The dividends paid as a % of profits were consistent with previous payments. The ex div market price was $5.50.

What will be the growth rate used to calculate the cost of equity for JS? Answers are given to 1 decimal place.

A   2.7%

B   5.3%

C   8.0%

D   16.9%

2.9 KR had originally acquired 75% of the 200,000 $1 issued ordinary shares of AP for $1,845,000 on 1 November 20X6, when the balance on AP's reserves was $2,040,000. No fair value adjustments were considered necessary to AP's net assets at the date of acquisition.

The current reporting date is 31 October 20X7 at which point AP's reserves were $3,000,000.

KR's profit for the year was $9,500,000.

Which of the following amounts will be shown within the consolidated statement of changes in equity?

	Parent shareholders	$000	Non-controlling interest	$000
A	Profit for the year	10,220	Profit for the year	240
B	Profit for the year	9,500	Profit for the year	240
C	Profit for the year	10,460	Profit for the year	0
D	Profit for the year	9,500	Profit for the year	960

2.10 NCI in the LA group at 1 January 20X8 was $525,000. The NCI share of total comprehensive income for the year ended 31 December 20X8 was $201,000. A 90% subsidiary was acquired during the year for proceeds of $750,000. NCI for this subsidiary is valued at fair value and on the acquisition date the carrying amount was $64,500. NCI on 31 December 20X8 is $603,000.

OBJECTIVE TEST QUESTIONS : SECTION 1

What is the cash flow related to NCI that should be shown in the consolidated statement of cash flows of the LA group for the year ended 31 December 20X8?

- A   A cash inflow of $750,000 in investing activities
- B   A cash outflow of $750,000 in investing activities
- C   A cash outflow of $214,500 in financing activities
- D   A cash inflow of $214,500 in financing activities
- E   A cash outflow of $187,500 in financing activities
- F   A cash inflow of $187,500 in investing activities
- G   A cash outflow of $58,500 in financing activities
- H   A cash inflow of $58,500 in financing activities

RANDOM QUESTION TEST 3

3.1 The following ratios have been calculated for two companies in the same industry, Company H and Company C.

	H	C
Current ratio	1.6	1.4
Quick ratio	1.2	1.1
Trade receivables days	52 days	69 days

Fill in the gaps using the options provided below to most accurately describe the liquidity of companies H and C.

more	Less
higher	Lower
longer	Shorter

H is _more_ liquid than C due to _higher_ levels of current assets compared to current liabilities.

C's liquidity could be improved if C could make its receivable days _shorter_.

3.2 NW has in issue 200,000 $100 par value convertible bonds. The bonds are redeemable at a premium of 10% or convertible into 12 shares in 3 years' time. The current share price is $8.50 and dividends are expected to grow at 4% per annum.

In order to calculate the cost of debt in relation to the bonds, an IRR calculation will be required.

What value should be included as the cash flow on redemption per bond within the internal rate of return calculation? Answers are given to the nearest $.

- A $100
- B $102
- C $110
- D $115

SUBJECT F2: ADVANCED FINANCIAL REPORTING

3.3 SJ acquired 80% of the equity share capital of DA on 1 January 20X6. SJ's presentational currency and functional currency is the $. DA presents its financial statements in the dinar.

At the date of acquisition, the carrying amount of DA's net assets was considered to be the same as the fair value (FV).

The carrying amount of DA's net assets in its financial statements at 31 December 20X8 is 3,000,000 dinars and its comprehensive income is 812,500 dinars.

Relevant exchange rates are as follows:

1 January 20X6 $1 = 15 dinar

31 December 20X7 $1 = 25 dinar

31 December 20X8 $1 = 20 dinar

Average rate for the year ended 31 December 20X8 $1 = 22 dinar

What is the annual exchange difference arising on the translation of the net assets of DA for inclusion in the SJ group financial statements for the year ended 31 December 20X8? No goodwill exchange impacts are required. Answers are given to the nearest $.

- A $6,932 loss
- B $6,932 gain
- C $25,568 loss
- D $25,568 gain
- E $32,762 loss
- F $32,762 gain

3.4 RX Ltd has issued 6% loan notes with a nominal value of $45,000 at 1 January 20X8.

Issue costs totalled $750. The effective interest rate for the loan notes is 8.5%.

What is the finance charge in the profit or loss account for the year ended 31 December 20X8 (to the nearest $)?

- A $2,673
- B $2,700
- C $3,761
- D $3,825

3.5 Moose Ltd leases an asset to a customer on 1 January 20X6. The lease term is for 5 years. The asset has an estimated useful life of 6 years and a current fair value of $89,000. The carrying amount of the asset at 1 January 20X6 is $70,000. The present value of the minimum lease payments is $87,000. Lease payments of $20,000 are made in arrears. The rate implicit with the lease is 4.8%

In accordance with IFRS 16, what is shown on the statement of financial positon as at the year ended 31 December 20X6?

- A Current receivable $20,000, Non-current receivable $50,216
- B Current receivable $16,584, Non-current receivable $54,592
- C Non-current receivable $70,216
- D Non-current receivable $71,176

OBJECTIVE TEST QUESTIONS : SECTION 1

3.6 LI has an 80% subsidiary, VE. LI also has an associate, RP with a 25% holding. During the year ended 31 December 20X6 the companies paid dividends of the following:

LI $1,800,000 ✓

VE $720,000

RP $360,000

What is the TOTAL for dividends paid in the consolidated statement of changes in equity of the LI group at 31 December 20X6?

A $2,466,000

B $2,376,000

C $1,944,000

D $1,800,000

Handwritten working:
1,800,000
(720 × 0.2) 144,000 NCI → the only part not intercompany
1,944,000

3.7 Which of the following would reasonably be expected to cause the **inventory days** of a company to decrease from one year to the next?

A Increased inventory obsolescence ✗

B Changing a key supplier

C Slowdown in trading

D A strategic decision to reduce selling prices ✗ → decrease inventory by selling more

Handwritten: ↓Inventory / ↑CofS × 365   Δ⁻

3.8 Which **two** of the following would be regarded as a **related party of JO**?

A HN, a major customer of JO

B The chief executive officer of the JO board ✓

C SH, an entity with which JO shares control of a joint venture

D AR, an entity in which the wife of the chief executive officer of the JO board has a controlling shareholding ✓

E TT, JO's main banker

3.9 An entity has the following sources of finance, together with their related costs:

	Nominal value	**Market value**	**Cost**
Equity	$5 million	$15 million	13.2%
Irredeemable debt	$5 million	$7.5 million	8.4%
Redeemable debt	$5 million	$10 million	9.6%

Handwritten: 32.5

What is the entity's weighted average cost of capital? Give your answer to 1 decimal place.

A 10.4%

B 10.8%

C 11.0%

D 11.3%

Handwritten working: 13.2% × 15/32.5 + 8.4% × 7.5/32.5 + 9.6% × 10/32.5
= 6.1% + 1.9% + 3.0%

81

SUBJECT F2: ADVANCED FINANCIAL REPORTING

3.10 On 1 January 20X3, CV acquired 70% of the equity share capital of LP for cash up-front of $5,625,000. The consideration also included a payment of an extra $3,000,000 that was dependent upon LP hitting a target return on capital employed by 31 December 20X4. The fair value of the contingent consideration at 1 January 20X3 was deemed $1,387,500.

The fair value of the net assets of LP on 1 January 20X3 was $3,750,000. It is group policy to value non-controlling interest (NCI) at fair value at the date of acquisition. The fair value of the NCI in LP on 1 January 20X3 was $1,800,000.

The goodwill arising on the acquisition of LP in the consolidated financial statements of the CV group at 1 January 20X3 is:

A $3,262,500
B $4,012,500
C $5,062,500
D $6,975,000

5,625,000 + 1,387,500
1,800,000
(3,750,000)
─────────
5,062,500

RANDOM QUESTION TEST 4

4.1 SH is a listed entity that operates in the technology sector, developing wristbands to monitor customer fitness levels and sporting performance. A competitor has developed a cheaper and less cumbersome product called Sporty Ring, to be worn around the customer's pinky finger. This has proven very popular and has seen SH's market share eroded in the last few months of 20X4, the financial period just ended.

Extracts from SH's financial information for the year are as follows:

	20X4	20X3
Revenue	$424m	$386m
Gross profit margin	22.4%	25.0%
Operating profit margin	4.2%	3.6%
Cash and cash equivalents	–	$12m
Short-term borrowings	$24m	–

Which one of the following statements is the most valid explanation for the reduction in gross profit margin that can be drawn from the above information and ratios?

A   A reduction in selling prices
B   A reduction in sales ×
C   An increase in cost prices ×
D   An increase in finance costs caused by the utilisation of an overdraft during 20X4 ×

4.2 HS is a listed entity that operates in the highly competitive technology sector

Extracts from HS's financial information for the year are as follows:

	20X4	20X3
Revenue	$429m	$388m
Current ratio CA/CL	1.5	2.2
Quick ratio CA-Inv/CL	0.8	1.5
Inventories holding period Inv/CofS × 365	50 days	80 days
Receivables collection period Rec/Sales × 365	32.5 days	30 days
Payables payment period Pay/CofS × 365	78 days	54.5 days

OBJECTIVE TEST QUESTIONS : SECTION 1

Which one of the following statements is a valid conclusion that can be drawn from the above ratios?

A   The decrease in inventory holding period has resulted in an increase in payable days

B   The decrease in inventory holding period has resulted in a fall in the quick ratio

C   The decrease in the inventory holding period has been caused by increased sales during the period

D   The decrease in inventory holding period has resulted in a fall in cost of sales

4.3 DA acquired 75% of the $1m ordinary share capital of VI for $5m on 31 January 20X8. The retained earnings of VI at this date were $3,650,000.

The carrying amount of the assets of VI were equal to fair value at the date of acquisition apart from an item of non-depreciable land that had a fair value $450,000 in excess of its carrying amount.

At the same date, DA acquired 30% of the $2m ordinary share capital of OB when the retained earnings of OB were $4,200,000. DA paid $8m for the shares of OB.

DA values goodwill using the fair value method. The fair value of the non-controlling interests on the 31 January 20X8 for VI was $1,650,000. Both investments were reviewed for impairment at the year end. In VI, no impairment of goodwill was deemed necessary. However, the investment in OB was impaired by $500,000.

The current reporting date is 31 January 20X9. Retained earnings for DA, VI and OB as at 31 January 20X9 are $10,800,000, $5,250,000 and $3,250,000 respectively.

What is the value of group retained earnings as at 31 January 20X9?

A $11,215,000

B $11,500,000

C $11,715,000

D $12,000,000

4.4 TS have just paid a dividend of 50 cents. The expected dividend growth rate is 7% and the cost of equity (ke) is 14.9%. The cum-div share price of TS is (to the nearest cent):

A $3.36

B $6.77

C $7.27

D $8.77

4.5 Mortimer had originally acquired 75% of the 1,000,000 $1 issued ordinary shares of Reeves on 1 November 20X6, when the balance on Reeves' reserves was $1,500,000. No fair value adjustments were considered necessary to Reeves' net assets at the date of acquisition.

The current reporting date is 31 October 20X7 at which point Reeves' reserves were $3,000,000.

Dividends of $1,000,000 were paid by Mortimer and Reeves during the year ended 20X7.

83

SUBJECT F2: ADVANCED FINANCIAL REPORTING

Which of the following amounts will be shown within the consolidated statement of changes in equity?

	Parent shareholders	$000	Non-controlling interest	$000
A	Dividend paid	1,000	Dividend paid	250
B	Dividend paid	1,750	Dividend paid	250
C	Dividend paid	1,000	Dividend paid	1,000
D	Dividend paid	1,750	Dividend paid	1,000

4.6 CD invested $2.56 million in corporate bonds on 1 January 20X6. It paid commission of 0.5% on the transaction and it plans to retain the investment until the fixed redemption date of 31 December 20X9. This is in line with the strategy used for all of CD's debt financial assets.

The journal entry to record the transaction on 1 January 20X6 is:

A	Dr	Bank	$2,547,200
	Cr	Financial liability	$2,547,200
B	Dr	Bank	$2,572,800
	Cr	Financial liability	$2,572,800
C	Dr	Financial asset	$2,547,200
	Cr	Bank	$2,547,200
D	Dr	Financial asset	$2,572,800
	Cr	Bank	$2,572,800
E	Dr	P/l	$12,800
	Dr	Financial asset	$2,560,000
	Cr	Cash	$2,572,800

4.7 Trump sells military equipment to Vlad, an entity based in Moldovia where the currency is the Moldovian pound (Mol). The equipment was sold on 1 October 20X1 for Mol 400,000. Vlad paid on 4 February 20X2. Trump's year end is 31 March 20X2.

Relevant rates are as follows:

1 October 20X1   US$1/Mol 1.65

4 February 20X2   US$1/ Mol 1.91

31 Mar 20X2   US$1/Mol 1.86

What is the exchange gain or loss when the payment is made in February 20X2?

A   Gain of $5,630

B   Loss of $5,630

C   Gain of $27,370

D   Loss of $27,370

E   Gain of $33,000

F   Loss of $33.000

OBJECTIVE TEST QUESTIONS : SECTION 1

4.8 On 30 June 20X4, HI acquired 800,000 of KL's 1 million shares. The purchase consideration was as follows:

HI issued three new shares for every four shares acquired in KL. On 30 June 20X4, the market price of a HI share was $3.80 and the market price of a KL share was $3.00.

HI agreed to pay $550,055 in cash to the existing shareholders on 30 June 20X5. HI's borrowing rate was 10% per annum.

HI paid advisors $100,000 for advice on the acquisition. → expense P&L.

What is the cost of investment that will be used in the goodwill calculation in the consolidated accounts of HI?

- A $2,400,000
- B $2,780,000
- C $2,830,000
- D $2,880,000

Cash PV = $500,050.
Shares = 600,000 × 3.8 = $2,280,000

2,780,050

4.9 Select which **two** of the following statements are correct for a company listed on a stock exchange

- A A stock exchange listing enables an exact valuation of the company on any given day. ✗ (market?)
- B Capital is more easily accessible for a company listed on a stock exchange. ?
- C The process of gaining a listing is straightforward and inexpensive. – expensive and time consuming
- D Grater reporting requirements are necessary for a public listed company. ✓
- E The original owners retain their control in the company when it floats on a stock exchange.

4.10 Which one of the following statements regarding the consolidated statement of cash flows is true?

- A Impairment of goodwill is not a cash inflow or outflow and, as such, does not affect the consolidated cash flow statement ✓ PAT.
- B The gross amount of cash paid to acquire a subsidiary during the year is always shown under 'cash flows from investing activities'. Gross paid – the cash held at $ at acq.
- C The dividend received from associates will be adjusted as part of the reconciliation to calculate 'cash generated from operations' Investing
- D Dividends paid to non-controlling interests will be presented under 'cash flows from financing activities' on the face of the consolidated cash flow statement ✗

SUBJECT F2: ADVANCED FINANCIAL REPORTING

RANDOM QUESTION TEST 5

5.1 LS acquired 75% of the $1m ordinary share capital of IVY for $5m on 31 January 20X8. The retained earnings of IVY at this date were $3,650,000.

The carrying amount of the assets of IVY were equal to fair value at the date of acquisition apart from an item of non-depreciable land that had a fair value $450,000 in excess of its carrying amount.

LS values goodwill using the fair value method. The fair value of the non-controlling interests on the 31 January 20X8 for IVY was $1,650,000. No impairment of goodwill was deemed necessary.

What value of goodwill is included in the LS Group statement of financial position as at 31 January 20X9?

- A $900,000
- B $1,550,000
- C $1,800,000
- D $2,000,000

5.2 AD acquired 75% of the $2m ordinary share capital of IV for $10m on 31 January 20X4. The retained earnings of IV at this date were $7.3m.

The carrying amount of the assets of IV were equal to fair value at the date of acquisition apart from an item of non-depreciable land with a carrying amount of $1m and a fair value of $1.9m.

AD values goodwill using the fair value method. The fair value of the non-controlling interests on the 31 January 20X4 for IV was $3.3m. No impairment of goodwill was deemed necessary.

The current reporting date is 31 January 20X5. Retained earnings for AD and IV as at 31 January 20X5 are $21.6m and $10.5m respectively.

Non-controlling interest of the AD group as shown in AD's consolidated statement of financial position at 31 January 20X5 is:

- A $3.35m
- B $3.85m
- C $4.1m
- D $5.7m

5.3 DAD acquired 30% of the ordinary share capital of BO when the retained earnings of BO were $2,200,000. DAD paid $8m for the shares of BO.

The investment in BO was impaired by $500,000.

The current reporting date is 31 January 20X9. Retained earnings for DAD and BO as at 31 January 20X9 are $10,800,000 and $1,250,000 respectively.

What is the investment in associate balance as shown in DAD's consolidated statement of financial position as at 31 January 20X9?

A ~~$7,215,000~~   Cost of inv = 8,000,000
B $7,715,000   Δ net asset = (950,000 × 0.3%)
C $7,785,000   Impairm = (500,000)
D $8,285,000   ─────────────
                                    7,215,000 ✓

5.4 SH is a listed entity that operates in the technology sector, developing applications and software to monitor customer fitness levels and sporting performance. A competitor has developed a cheaper and more varied app that is compatible with the products produced by all the major tech brands. This has proven very popular and has seen SH's market share eroded in the last few months of the financial period just ended 20X4.

Extracts from SH's financial information for the year are as follows:

	20X4	20X3
Revenue	$848m	$772m g = 9.84%
Gross profit margin	22.4%	25.0%
Operating profit margin	4.2%	3.6%
Payables payment period Pay/cofs × 365	78 days	54.5 days
Cash and cash equivalents	–	$52m
Short-term borrowings	$18m	–

Which one of the following statements is a valid conclusion that can be drawn from the above ratios?

A   SH has increased its marketing expenditure during the year to combat the impact of the new product in the market ✗

(B)   SH operates in a marketplace that has shown growth in the last 12 months

~~C~~   The increase in payables payment period has been caused by an increase in the credit terms of SH's main suppliers ✓ → could it be by the lack of cash.

D   SH is insolvent as SH is overdrawn and its bank is looking for repayment of the overdraft ✗   * very strong

5.5 PH entered into an arrangement to lease a machine with a 3-year useful lifetime to a customer on 1 July 20X7 with the following terms:

- Three year non-cancellable lease
- An initial deposit of $5,000 is received
- Rent of $12,000 per annum payable
- Rate implicit with the lease of 10%
- The carrying amount of the machine was $20,000 as at 1 July 20X7

suggest it is a financial lease

Which of the following statements regarding the accounting of this lease arrangement is true?

A   The lease is an operating lease due to the relatively short lease term ✗

~~B~~   A lease receivable of $34,844 will be outstanding on the 1 July 20X7 · PV + deposit not correct

(C)   Profit of $14,844 is recorded on disposal of the machine

D   Interest income of $2,984 will be credited to profit or loss during the year ended 31 December 20X7 ✗ → just 6 months

SUBJECT F2: ADVANCED FINANCIAL REPORTING

5.6 Which of the following is not a limitation of applying ratio analysis to published financial statements?

    A   Accounting policy choices can limit comparability between different companies

    B   Financial statements may contain errors

    C   Information within published financial statements is historic and out of date

    D   Different ways of calculating certain ratios exist

5.7 Monkfish plc had profits after tax of $4.2 million in the year ended 31 December 20X7. On 1 January 20X7, Monkfish had 3.36 million ordinary shares in issue. On 1 April 20X7, Monkfish made a one for two rights issue at a price of $1.40 when the market price of Monkfish's shares was $2.00.

What is the basic earnings per share figure for the year ended 31 December 20X7, according to IAS 33 *Earnings per Share*?

    A   49.5 cents

    B   89.1 cents

    C   91.2 cents

    D   92.6 cents

5.8 BB has some 5% $100 loan notes in issue, which are redeemable in 3 years' time at a premium of 12.5%. The current market value of the loan notes is $98.

Using discount rates of 5% and 10%, calculate the yield to maturity (YTM) to two decimal places.

5.9 Which of the following statements regarding IAS 21 *The effects of changes in foreign exchange rates* is correct?

    A   All foreign currency transactions will be restated using the closing rate as at the reporting date

    B   Foreign currency gains or losses must be recorded within the statement of profit or loss

    C   The functional currency is the currency that must be used to present an entity's financial statements

    D   The statement of profit or loss of a foreign subsidiary would be translated using the average exchange rate for the period before consolidation within the group's accounts.

5.10 Integrated reporting outlines a number of types of capitals to represent the ways that value can be created within particular entities.

The value of capitals of an entity can be both increased and eroded as an entity operates.

An entity has had exceptionally high staff turnover for a number of years.

Under which of the following capitals would this issue be assigned within the entity's integrated report and would it be deemed to increase or decrease value?

	Type of capital	Impact on value
A	Human	Increase
B	Manufactured	Increase
C	Natural	Increase
D	Human	Decrease
E	Manufactured	Decrease
F	Natural	Decrease

Section 2

ANSWERS TO OBJECTIVE TEST QUESTIONS

FINANCING CAPITAL PROJECTS

LONG TERM FINANCE

1 **A, C**

  B – Debt instruments can also be traded in the capital markets.

  D – An unlisted entity can issue shares, but not on the stock market e.g. by using a rights issue to existing shareholders.

  E – The primary function is to enable entities to raise finance, enabling investors to buy and sell investments is the secondary function.

2 **General assets, less preferable**

A floating charge is when debt is secured against **general assets** of the entity and this type of charge is considered **less preferable** to a fixed charge from the lenders point of view.

3 **A**

  B – Raising finance via a rights issue does not cause the flotation of an entity. Non-listed entities can issue rights issues to their current private shareholders. Flotation (being a publically listed entity) is not required to raise finance via a rights issue.

  C – Rights issues are made in proportion to shareholders' existing holdings therefore do not result in a dilution to the percentage ownership if fully subscribed.

  D – A rights issue is offered to all shareholders.

4 **D**

Theoretical ex rights price = $\dfrac{(5 \times \$2.75) + \$2.25}{6}$ = $2.67

5 **Cum rights, ex rights**

When a rights issue is announced, the existing shares will be traded **cum rights** up to the date of the issue. After the issue takes place, the shares will then be traded **ex rights**.

SUBJECT F2: ADVANCED FINANCIAL REPORTING

6 D

The directors are required to pay the preference dividend if sufficient distributable profits are available.

7 C, D

C – Preference shareholders would be paid dividends in preference to ordinary shareholders.

D – Ordinary dividends are not a fixed amount, they are determined by the directors.

8 $7.31

Theoretical ex rights price = $\dfrac{(3 \times \$7.50) + \$6.75}{4} = \$7.31$

9 D

The liability component of convertible debt must be recognised in the statement of financial position.

10 More, uncertainty, equity, debt

The providers of equity finance face **more** risk than the providers of debt finance because there is greater **uncertainty** over the level of their return. As a result, **equity** providers will require a higher level of return on their investment than **debt** providers.

COST OF CAPITAL AND YIELD TO MATURITY

11 8.7%

$k_e = \dfrac{0.60}{(7.50 - 0.60)} = 8.7\%$

12 D

$k_e = \dfrac{0.10 \times 1.03}{\text{ex-div price}} + 0.03 = 0.15$

Therefore, ex-div price = $\dfrac{0.10 \times 1.03}{0.15 - 0.03} = \$0.86 = 86$ cents

13 Ex div market price

When calculating the cost of preference shares, the dividend is divided by the **ex div market price** of the preference share.

14 6.3%

Yield to maturity = $6/94.5 \times 100 = 6.3\%$

ANSWERS TO OBJECTIVE TEST QUESTIONS : SECTION 2

15 8.9%

$$k_e = \frac{0.10 \times 1.03}{1.86 - 0.10} + 0.03 = 8.9\%$$

16 $109.50

Cash conversion = $100 × 102% = $102

Shares conversion = 15 × ($6 × 1.04^5) = $109.50

Assume that investor will choose the higher value option.

17 B

Post-tax cost of debt = (5 × 80%)/88 = 4.5%

18 B

The relevant cash outflows would be the annual interest payment **net of tax**, not gross, and the redemption value.

19 7.5%

Yield to maturity = 7/92.75 × 100 = 7.5%

20 A

$$k_e = \frac{divi \times 1.04}{6.50} + 0.04 = 0.125$$

$$\text{Therefore, divi} = \frac{(0.125 - 0.04) \times 6.50}{1.04} = 0.53$$

21 $2.73

$$k_e = \frac{0.13 \times 1.05}{\text{current price}} + 0.05 = 0.10$$

$$\text{Therefore, current price} = \frac{0.13 \times 1.05}{0.10 - 0.05} = 2.73$$

22 4.1%

Post-tax cost of debt = (6 × 70%)/102 = 4.1%

23 D

Cash option = $100 × 115% = $115

Shares option = 10 × ($10.22 × 1.02^5) = $112.84

Assume that the investor will choose the higher value option.

24 13.2%

WACC = (15% × 4/5) + (8% × 75% × 1/5) = 12% + 1.2% = 13.2%

The yield on debt is 8%. This is gross of tax. Cost of debt (required for WACC calculations) is net of tax. As the debt is irredeemable, the cost of debt is 75% (1-25%) of the yield.

25 D

Source	Market value $m	Proportion	Cost of capital %	Weighted cost %
Ordinary shares (10 × 1.20)	12	0.632	11.7	7.4
Long-dated bonds (8 × 0.875)	7	0.368	6	2.2
	19	1		9.6

26 D

$K_d = (7 \times 70\%)/96 = 5.1\%$

$K_e = 0.50 / (3.80 - 0.50) = 15.2\%$

27 6%

Post-tax cost of debt = (coupon rate × 75%)/92 = 4.89%

Therefore, coupon rate = 0.0489 × 92/0.75 = 6%

28 C

$$k_e = \frac{0.12 \times 1.05}{1.22} + 0.05 = 15.3\%$$

Dividend per share in above calculation = 120,000/1m = 0.12

29 C

A, B and D are all considered to be benefits/uses of WACC.

C is a limitation as the WACC should ideally reflect market values.

30 8.7%

$$\text{Yield to maturity (IRR)} = 5\% + \frac{12.91}{(12.91 + 4.65)} \times (10\% - 5\%) = 8.7\%$$

ANSWERS TO OBJECTIVE TEST QUESTIONS : SECTION 2

FINANCIAL REPORTING STANDARDS

IAS 32 & IFRS 9 *FINANCIAL INSTRUMENTS*

31 Asset, equity, obligation, unfavourable

'A financial instrument is any contract that gives rise to a financial **asset** of one entity and a financial liability or **equity** instrument of another entity.

A financial liability is any liability that is a contractual **obligation** to deliver cash or another financial asset to another entity or to exchange financial assets or liabilities under **unfavourable** conditions '(IAS 32, para 11).

32 B

Finance costs recognised by ROB are:

	$
Issue costs	100,000
Interest paid (4m × 5%)	200,000
	300,000

The finance costs that should have been recognised are:

	$
(4m – 100,000) × 8.5%	331,500

Therefore, the journal entry to correct the current accounting treatment is:

			$
Dr	Finance costs		31,500
Cr	Liability		31,500

33 $9,342,264

Initial recognition of the liability will be calculated as the total cash received less equity component.

Liability should then be subsequently measured at amortised cost.

	$
Opening liability (10m – 794,200)	9,205,800
Finance cost at effective rate (9,205,800 × 8%)	736,464
Cash paid (10m × 6%)	(600,000)
Liability at 31 December 20X3	9,342,264

SUBJECT F2: ADVANCED FINANCIAL REPORTING

34 **$5,840**

	$
Initial measurement at acquisition (40,000 × $2.68 × 1.05)	112,560
Fair value at 31 July 20X2 (40,000 × $2.96)	118,400
Gain	5,840

Transaction costs are added to FVOCI financial assets upon initial recognition.

35 The liability for this instrument at 31 December 20X1 will be calculated as follows:

Liability		$
Opening balance	(3.4m – 200,000)	**3,200,000**
Plus: finance cost	(3.2m × 7.05%)	**225,600**
Less: interest paid	(3.4m × 6%)	**(204,000)**
Closing balance		X

36 **B**

A is not appropriate as the loans to employees are not held for trading purposes.

C is not appropriate as the loans to employees are not held with the intention to hold some and sell some of the loans.

D is not appropriate as the loans are financial assets, not financial liabilities.

37 **D**

Cumulative preference shares should be recognised as a financial liability as there is an obligation to pay the dividends (due to them being cumulative). Therefore, A is incorrect and D would be correct. The dividend paid would be recorded as finance costs to match the treatment of the instrument as a liability.

Cumulative preference shares allow dividends to be deferred and paid cumulatively in periods of poor liquidity. Non-cumulative irredeemable preference shares would lose their right to dividend if AB decided to forego a dividend payment. Cumulative preference shares are less risky than non-cumulative preference shares. Therefore, B is incorrect.

AB has issued the preference shares in order to raise finance, rather than acquiring them as an investment. Therefore, C is incorrect.

38 D

Upon disposal of FVOCI equity financial assets, any gains held in reserves cannot be recycled to the statement of profit or loss. The gains must remain in equity, most likely through recycling through retained earnings.

Equity financial assets can be irrevocably designated as FVOCI. Option A is incorrect.

As the financial asset has been disposed of by the 31 December 20X3, the FVOCI financial asset would be derecognised and, as such, the carrying amount at that point would be 0. Option B is incorrect.

A gain of $18,000 would be held in reserves as at 31 December 20X2. Option C is incorrect.

39 The journal entry required to record the subsequent measurement of the shares at 31 December 20X1 is:

	Account reference	$
Debit	Investment in shares	310,000
Credit	**Profit or loss**	

Transaction costs are expensed upon initial recognition of a held for trading (fair value through profit or loss) equity financial asset.

40 A

	$
Contracted purchase price (1,000 × $1,200)	1,200,000
Equivalent purchase price at reporting date (1,000 × $1,280)	1,280,000
Gain on contract (therefore, favourable terms)	80,000

41 C

As RF has purchased the convertible bonds, RF will record a financial asset.

The financial asset will include contractual cash flows that compensate the issuer for providing the holder the right to convert into shares. Consequently, the contractual cash flows test is not adhered to as all cash flows do not relate solely to interest and capital repayments. The financial asset must be classified as fair value through profit or loss (FVPL).

Convertible bonds are split between liability and equity elements from the issuer's perspective, not the holder's. Option A is incorrect.

Interest in the profit or loss account will be determined based upon the effective interest rate associated with the bond. As the bond would be redeemed at a premium, the effective interest rate would be greater than the coupon of 5%. The coupon rate multiplied by the par value gives $500,000. This would be the cash flow received, not the expense recorded. Options B and D are incorrect.

42 B

The preference shares are redeemable and should, therefore, be classified as a financial liability.

Issue costs are deducted from the initial recognition of the redeemable preference shares.

	$
Cash received	5,000,000
Less, issue costs incurred	(200,000)
Initial measurement of preference shares	4,800,000

The correct journal entry to correct the accounting treatment is:

		$
Dr	Bank	4,800,000
Cr	Financial liability	4,800,000

43 C

The investment is a financial asset which would be measured at amortised cost. MAT's intention is to hold until the maturity date, passing the business model test. All cash flows are capital and interest, passing the contractual cash flow test. Any transaction costs should be added to the asset on initial recognition.

	$
Amount paid for investment	2,000,000
Transaction costs incurred	100,000
Initial measurement of financial asset	2,100,000

The journal entry to correct the accounting treatment is:

		$
Dr	Investment	2,100,000
Cr	Bank	2,100,000

44 B

	$
PV of principal after 4 years = $6m × 0.708	4,248,000
PV of interest of 7% on $6m for 4 years = $6m × 7% × 3.24	1,360,800
Initial measurement of liability component	5,608,800

Equity = $6m − $5,608,800 = $391,200

Discount factors use the prevailing market rate of interest for similar debt without conversion rights which was 9%.

ANSWERS TO OBJECTIVE TEST QUESTIONS : SECTION 2

45 D

	A$
Contracted purchase price (2m/0.64)	3,125,000
Equivalent purchase price at reporting date (2m/0.70)	2,857,143
Loss on contract (therefore unfavourable terms)	267,857

46 The impact of the investment in the statement of profit or loss for the year ended 30 June 20X1 is:

Statement of profit or loss extract	$
Profit from operations	X
Finance income (4.2m × 8.4%)	**352,800**
Finance costs	**BLANK**
	———
Profit before tax	X

The debt instrument is classified as amortised cost as the business intends to hold its debt financial assets.

Initial recognition of the financial asset will be at fair value (typically cost) plus any transaction costs. For this amortised cost debt financial asset = $4,000,000 + $200,000 = $4,200,000.

The subsequent treatment of the financial asset is to value at amortised cost.

As this is a debt instrument, finance income and coupon rate receipts will need to be recorded.

The effective rate applied to the opening measurement will calculate finance income as the investment is a financial asset (not a financial liability).

To work out entries to record the debt financial asset, the following working will be required:

B/f	Interest at effective rate (8.4%)	Receipt at coupon (7%)	Amortised cost
4,200,000	352,800	(280,000)	4,272,800

47 The journal entry required to record the subsequent measurement of the investment at 30 June 20X2 is:

	Account reference	$
Debit	Investment in shares	122,000
Credit	Reserves	

The investment is classified as FVOCI. As a result, transaction costs are added to the asset at initial recognition. Subsequent measurement is at fair value with changes in value being recorded in reserves.

	$
Initial recognition of investment (2,400,000 × 1.02)	2,448,000
Fair value at reporting date	2,570,000
Gain on re-measurement	122,000

48 The journal entry required to initially record the convertible bond on 1 January 20X2 is:

	Account reference	$
Debit	Bank	4,000,000
Credit	Financial liability	3,689,200
Credit	Equity	310,800

Tutorial note:

The calculation of the liability and equity component is provided below, however you would not need to perform this calculation to answer the question. A convertible bond is part liability and part equity and the liability component will always be the higher of the two values – if you know this, then there is only one valid option which is to include 3,689,200 as the liability component and 310,800 as the equity component.

Calculation (as proof of figures)

	$
PV of principal after 5 years = $4m × 0.65	2,600,000
PV of interest of 7% on $4m for 5 years = $4m × 7% × 3.89	1,089,200
Initial measurement of liability component	3,689,200

Equity component = $4m − $3,689,200 = $310,800

IAS 33 *EARNINGS PER SHARE*

49 50.7 cents

Basic EPS = $3.8m/(5m × 3/2) = 50.7 cents

50 B

Earnings = $6,582,000 − $420,000 = $6,162,000

Weighted average number of shares:

Brought forward	8,000,000
Market price issue (5/12 × 2,400,000)	1,000,000
	9,000,000

Basic EPS = $6,162,000/9,000,000 = 68.5 cents

51 3,694,349

Weighted average number of shares:

Prior to rights issue	3m × 1/12 × 7.5/7.3	256,849
After rights issue	3m × 5/4 × 11/12	3,437,500
		3,694,349

The rights issue bonus fraction is cum rights price/theoretical ex rights price. Cum rights price is the price immediately before the rights issue of $7.50. The subsequent increase in share price is irrelevant.

52 D

Dilutive shares:	
Share held under option	1,000,000
Shares as if issued at market price ((1m × 3.1)/4)	(775,000)
Shares effectively issued for no consideration	225,000

Diluted EPS = $3.5m/(7m + 225,000) = 48.4 cents

53 $862,500

Weighted average number of shares:

Brought forward	10,000,000	
Market price issue (9/12 × 2,000,000)	1,500,000	
		11,500,000
Bonus issue		× 5/4
		14,375,000

Basic EPS = 6 cents = profit/14,375,000

Therefore, profit = 14,375,000 × $0.06 = $862,500

SUBJECT F2: ADVANCED FINANCIAL REPORTING

54 28.8 cents

Adjusted earnings:	$
Per basic eps	3,000,000
Interest on convertible instrument ($5m × 6% × 75%)	225,000
	3,225,000

Diluted EPS = $3,225,000/(10m + 1.2m) = 28.8 cents

55 A, D

Irredeemable preference dividends relating to previous years will have been deducted from previous years' earnings. Therefore, B is incorrect.

Ordinary dividends are distributions of earnings and, as such, are not part of the calculation to find earnings. Therefore, C is incorrect.

Redeemable preference dividends will be recognised as a finance cost within profit or loss and, therefore, will already be reflected in the profit after tax figure.

56 B

Comparative EPS = last years' EPS × rights bonus fraction inverted

Rights bonus fraction = CRP/TERP = 2.2/2.06

Therefore, comparative EPS = 46.2 cents × 2.06/2.2 = 43.3 cents

57 78.6 cents

Comparative EPS = last years' EPS × bonus fraction inverted

There is no restatement with respect to a full market price issue.

Therefore, comparative EPS = 98.2 cents × 4/5 = 78.6 cents

58 B

Dilutive shares:	
Share held under option	1,500,000
Shares that would have been issued at market price ((1.5m × 3.5)/4.75)	(1,105,263)
Shares effectively issued for no consideration	394,737

IFRS 16 *LEASES*

59 For a lessor, an asset leased on an **operating** lease would be held within the statement of financial position, and **rental** income is subsequently recognised within **the statement of profit or loss.**

ANSWERS TO OBJECTIVE TEST QUESTIONS : SECTION 2

60 B

The rental income in relation to an operating lease should be recorded in the statement of profit or loss on a straight-line basis over the lease term.

The total amount to be paid is $45,000 (30 months × $1,500 as Hudson receives $1,500 a month for 3 years, less the first six-month rent-free period).

This would be spread across the 3-year lease period, giving a rental income of $15,000 a year. As the lease was only agreed six months into the year, only six months rental income should be recorded in 20X7. This gives a rental income of $7,500 for the year end 31 December 20X7.

As nothing has been paid by the year end, an accrued income balance of $7,500 would also be shown in the statement of financial position.

61 A, C, E

In accordance with IFRS 16 *Leases*, lessors must consider whether a lease is a finance lease or an operating lease. A finance lease is one in which the significant risks and rewards of ownership of the leased asset have transferred to the lessee.

If the lessor (FL) is responsible for maintenance and repair this would suggest that the risk of damage and breakdown has not been transferred to the lessee (JS). Therefore, B is incorrect.

The sale at the end of the lease is at normal commercial terms. Being able to buy the asset at market value does not suggest either a risk or reward of ownership. There is no benefit or downside from the condition. Therefore, D is not an indicator of risk or reward transfer and, consequently, of the presence of a finance lease.

62 B

	B/f	Interest 7%	Payment	c/f
	$	$	$	$
31/10/X3	30,000	2,100	(7,317)	24,783
31/10/X4	24,783	1,735	(7,317)	19,201

The figure to the right of the payment in the next year is the non-current receivable.

63 A, D, E

The lease in question is a finance lease. The risk and rewards are transferred to the lessee. This can be determined as the lease term is the majority of the asset's useful lifetime and the present value of the lease payments will make up significantly all of the asset's fair value.

When a lessor enters into a finance lease with a customer it will:

- derecognise the leased asset (in this case, from PPE)
- record a lease receivable at the net investment in the lease
- record a gain or loss on disposal.

Rental receipts and interest income are recorded subsequently. The rental receipts are recorded in cash and by reducing the lease receivable. The interest income is recorded in profit or loss and increases the lease receivable. These balances are unaffected at the initial point of recording the lease (1 December 20X9).

Right-of-use assets are relevant to lessee accounting and not lessor accounting.

SUBJECT F2: ADVANCED FINANCIAL REPORTING

IFRS 15 REVENUE FROM CONTRACTS WITH CUSTOMERS

64 A, E

For revenue to be recorded, a contract must exist and the distinct performance obligations of the contract must be identified.

Performance obligations do not always need to be fully satisfied for revenue to be recorded. If performance obligations are satisfied over time, revenue from the contract can be allocated across a period of time. Option B is incorrect.

Variable consideration can be included within revenue if it is highly probable to not reverse. It is not a requirement for revenue to be recorded. Every contract does not need an element of variable consideration. Option C is incorrect.

It is the transfer of control, rather than the delivery itself, that are conditions that must be satisfied in accordance with IFRS 15. It is possible for no control transfer to have occurred despite the goods already being delivered e.g. sale or return arrangements. D is not always correct.

65 C

'If a sale includes a significant financing element, revenue is limited to the present value discounted at the seller's rate of borrowing' is the correct statement.

Variable consideration is only included in the contract price if it is highly probable that a significant reversal in the amount of cumulative revenue will not occur.

Revenue is recorded as performance obligations are satisfied by the seller (either at a point in time or over time). It is not directly linked to the recognition of cash.

Non-cash consideration is included in revenue at the fair value of the non-cash consideration, not the cost of the sold goods.

66 B

Revenue can be recorded over time if the customer simultaneously receives and consumes the benefits provided by the seller. The support service would meet this condition and be recorded over the 3 years that the support is provided.

Revenue is recorded at a point in time if control of the good is transferred to the customer. As a result of the software being developed and delivered on 30 June 20X3, then revenue is recorded in full at that date.

	$
Revenue from sale of goods (software)	500,000
Revenue from provision of service (75,000/3 years × 6/12)	12,500
Total revenue to be recognised in year ended 31 December 20X3	512,500

ANSWERS TO OBJECTIVE TEST QUESTIONS : SECTION 2

67 B

As the customer will take 3 years to pay and a difference between the cash price and the repayment exists, this contract includes a significant financing element.

The discount factor for $1 receivable in 3 years' time with a 7% interest rate is 0.816.

The revenue from sale of the goods is the present value of the amount receivable in 3 years' time, which equals $4,896 (6,000 × 0.816).

| Dr Receivable | $4,896 |
| Cr Revenue | $4,896 |

68 B

Half-a-job Bob is working as an agent matching manual labour/building work requests, submitted by the users of the website, to relevant local professionals, who perform the work. Half-a-job Bob performs none of the labour required but charges a commission for facilitating the work. Half-a-job Bob simply arrange for another party to provide the services and so it is an agent. Agents can only record revenue up to the amount of commission they earn. Revenue of $1m is recorded by Half-a-job Bob ($10m × 10%).

The amount of paid fees is irrelevant with regard to recognising revenue. $1m is still recorded as revenue despite only $0.9m being received in cash.

69 C

The revenue from the sale of goods from XZ to WY would be recorded at a point in time. The revenue should only be recognised when control of the goods has transferred to WY. Control of the goods transfers to WY on delivery.

The right to return means a refund liability will be required of 10% of the sales value. The refund liability would equal $125,000 (being $1,250,000 × 10%). Revenue would be limited to $1,125,000 (being $1,250,000 – $125,000).

There is no significant finance component in this sale as the credit terms are not long enough. A is incorrect.

As stated above, control transfers on delivery and revenue is recorded at that point in time. B is incorrect.

Inventory would be derecognised by XZ as control is transferred. D is incorrect.

70 $1.9M

In 20X1:

Total expected profit = 40m – 7m – 26m = $7 million

Stage of completion = 8/40 = 20%

Profit recognised = 20% × $7m = $1.4 million

In 20X2:

Total expected profit = 40m – 18m – 16m = $6 million

Stage of completion = 22/40 = 55%

Cumulative profit to be recognised = 55% × $6m = $3.3 million

Therefore, profit to be recognised in 20X2 = $3.3m – $1.4m = **$1.9 million**

SUBJECT F2: ADVANCED FINANCIAL REPORTING

71 D

The 5 step process for recording revenue as per IFRS 15 is:

1   Identify the contract
2   Identify the separate performance obligations within a contract
3   Determine the transaction price
4   Allocate the transaction price to the performance obligations in the contract
5   Recognise revenue when (or as) a performance obligation is satisfied.

As per the 5 steps, revenue is recognised when the performance obligations are satisfied. This could be at a point in time or over time. The transfer of control is an indicator as to when performance obligations are satisfied at a point in time. Transfer of control is not highlighted directly as a separate step within the 5 step process.

72 B

	$000	$000
Contract price		3,000
Costs:		
Incurred to date – re work completed	1,500	
Inventory not yet used	150	
To complete	350	
		(2,000)
Total expected profit		1,000

Percentage complete = 1,500/2,000 = 75%

Therefore, profit = 75% × $1,000,000 = $750,000

73 A

	$m
Contract price	26
Costs incurred to date	(17)
Costs to complete	(11)
Expected loss	(2)

This is a loss making contract, therefore, the statement of profit or loss extract would show the total loss immediately. Extracts from the statement of profit or loss would be as follows:

	$m
Revenue (= work certified)	14
Cost of sales (balancing figure)	(16)
Loss	(2)

ANSWERS TO OBJECTIVE TEST QUESTIONS : SECTION 2

IAS 37 *PROVISIONS, CONTINGENT LIABILITIES AND CONTINGENT ASSETS*

74 C

Future operating losses are specifically prohibited by IAS 37 *Provisions, contingent liabilities and contingent assets*. No provision should be made as there is no obligation.

75 D

If ES have created a valid expectation that ES will incur costs to clean-up such leaks in its environmental and social report, ES will have created a constructive obligation and, therefore, should make a provision. The leak has already occurred therefore there is a past event giving rise to the obligation.

A is incorrect as there does not have to be a legal obligation; it could be a constructive obligation instead as discussed above.

B is incorrect as an estimate has been made of the costs and, therefore, provided there is an obligation, a provision would be required rather than a contingent liability.

C is incorrect as an intention is not sufficient to make a provision; there must be an obligation.

76 The IAS 37 *Provisions, contingent liabilities and contingent assets* accounting treatment can be summarised as follows:

Degree of probability of an outflow/inflow of resources	Liability	Asset
Virtually certain	Recognise	Recognise
Probable	Make provision	Disclose (in note)
Possible	Disclose (in note)	Ignore
Remote	Ignore	Ignore

IAS 38 *INTANGIBLE ASSETS*

77 C, E, F

Although the other three items are similar to the criteria, they are not specific enough.

Probable economic benefit must be generated. The benefits are not restricted to simply revenue generation.

Costs must be measured reliably, not just measured.

The criteria of the standard states adequate resources, not just adequate cash.

78 A

Research costs are expensed to the statement of profit or loss as per IAS 38.

The purchased goodwill, brand name and the development costs are all intangible assets.

79 D

The options present items of research or development expenditure incurred during various projects. Research should be expensed in the profit or loss. Development costs are capitalised under intangible assets.

To be considered as development costs, the following factors are required to be met:

Probable future economic benefit is expected from the project

Intention to use/sell the asset

Resources are available to complete the project

Ability to use/sell the asset

Technically feasible

Expenditure can be reliably identified and measured.

Option A cannot be capitalised because it is not effective currently so cannot be feasible and will not be expected to generate economic benefit.

Option B is clearly research.

Option C fails to generate future economic benefit (it is loss making) so cannot be deemed to be development costs.

80 B

An intangible is an identifiable asset without physical substance. To meet the recognition criteria from the Framework, the transaction must meet a definition of an element (an asset in this case), and be relevant and show a faithful representation. The definition of an asset, is a resource controlled by the entity as a result of a past event from which future economic benefit are expected to flow to the entity.

To be identifiable, an asset must be capable of being disposed of separately from other assets.

Sybil has purchased a subsidiary, Basil, which owns a brand name and a customer list. The brand is reliably valued at $500,000 and so recognition provides a faithful representation, so this should be accounted for as a separate intangible asset on consolidation.

The customer list cannot be valued reliably, and so will form part of the overall goodwill calculation. It will be subsumed within the goodwill value recorded on consolidation.

81 B

A new process may produce benefits other than increased revenues and can still be capitalised, e.g. it may reduce costs.

Revaluation of intangibles can occur if the intangible can be reliably measured. To be reliably measured intangible assets will be sold in an active market. For intangible assets, this is rare but not unheard of (e.g. taxi cab licences). Therefore, revaluation is permissible for intangible assets.

Internally generated intangibles are not capitalised. Only purchased intangibles or development costs can be recorded within the statement of financial position.

Goodwill is treated under IFRS 3 *Business combinations* and not IAS 38 *Intangible assets*. As a result, it is not amortised. It is reviewed for impairment annually.

ANSWERS TO OBJECTIVE TEST QUESTIONS : SECTION 2

IAS 12 TAXATION

82 A, C

In the other three situations, the carrying amount of the asset is greater than its tax base and, therefore, a deferred tax liability exists.

83 B

Deferred tax liability at 31 December 20X3 = (470,000 – 365,000) × 20% = $21,000

Therefore, there is a reduction in deferred tax liability in the year of $4,000 => credit in profit or loss.

84 B, C, D

The additional temporary difference created by the revaluation is $350,000. The additional deferred tax liability arising on this is $70,000. Therefore, A is incorrect.

	Before revaluation $000	After revaluation $000
Carrying amount of PPE	400	750
Tax base	(370)	(370)
Temporary difference	30	380
Deferred tax liability at 20%	6	76

The increase in liability from $4,000 (b/f) to $6,000 (above) is charged to profit or loss.

The additional $70,000 created by the revaluation is charged to other comprehensive income and debited to the revaluation surplus.

Therefore, the balance on the revaluation surplus = 350,000 – 70,000 = $280,000

85 D

There is a deductible temporary difference resulting in a deferred tax asset (not a liability) which can be recognised based upon amounts reasonably expected to be realised in the future. The temporary difference multiplied by the tax rate would give the deferred tax asset value as shown within the statement of financial position.

86 Taxable, liability

If the carrying amount of an asset exceeds its tax base, then there is a **taxable** temporary difference and this will result in a deferred tax **liability**.

SUBJECT F2: ADVANCED FINANCIAL REPORTING

IAS 24 *RELATED PARTIES*

87 A, B, F

The above are specifically defined as related parties.

C and D are specifically excluded from the definition of a related party.

Employees would not be considered to be a related party unless they were members of key management personnel.

88 B

Subsidiaries, associates and joint ventures are all related parties.

Two venturers who have joint control of an entity are excluded from the definition, therefore, AB and PQ would not be considered to be related parties.

IAS 21 *FOREIGN CURRENCY TRANSACTIONS*

89 D

The sale is recorded at the exchange rate of £400,000/0.65 = $615,385 giving a journal of Dr Receivables Cr Revenue.

90 On receipt of the payment from the customer, the entity will record a foreign currency **gain** of **$44,118** which will be recorded within **profit or loss**.

Workings

The sale is initially recorded at historic rate of $1: €0.85. A receivable of $705,882 is recorded.

The payment is recorded at the exchange rate when the cash was received €600,000/0.80 = $750,000. This amount is debited to the bank.

The receivables will be credited with $705,882 to remove the amount initially recorded. The difference of $44,118 will be credited to the statement of profit or loss as a gain.

91 IAS 21 *The Effects of Changes in Foreign Exchange Rates* states unsettled **monetary** items, e.g. receivables, must be **retranslated using the closing rate** at the reporting date and **non-monetary** items are **left at historical rate**.

92 D

Functional currency is defined as the currency of the primary economic environment in which an entity operates.

93 C

The foreign currency transaction would initially be recorded at historic rate. This is the rate when Sunshine bought the land (30 June 20X1). Land and a payable are recorded at $10m (30m dinars/3).

At the year end, the payable would be restated to closing rate as it is a monetary liability (2 dinars/$). The payable should now be valued at $15m being a movement of $5m. The foreign currency loss is recorded in profit or loss. Therefore, Dr profit or loss $5m Cr payables $5m.

The non-monetary asset is not revalued at the year end.

94 A

Overseas transactions are recorded in the functional currency using the spot rate of exchange. Therefore, the land is initially recorded at $5 million (15m dinars/3).

Land is a non-monetary asset and so is not retranslated. It is also not depreciated. Its carrying amount remains at $5 million as at the year end.

GROUP ACCOUNTS

SUBSIDIARIES

95 C

Although the transaction would not affect the consolidated financial statements, it would affect the subsidiary's individual financial statements and is an attempt to mislead any potential acquirers.

The transaction would have to be disclosed as a related party transaction. For users to understand the impact of the transaction on profit they would need to be made aware of the inflated prices, however LP are not planning to disclose any information about the price increase.

96 C

In accordance with IFRS 3 *Business* combinations, any contingent consideration should be recognised at fair value in the goodwill calculation.

Tutorial note:
The extent of probability would be reflected in the fair value of the contingent consideration.

SUBJECT F2: ADVANCED FINANCIAL REPORTING

97 D

	$000
Carrying amount	850
Fair value uplift to PPE	650
Fair value uplift to inventory	25
Contingent liability	(100)
Fair value of net assets at acquisition	1,425

98 A

The fair value adjustment is subjected to extra depreciation and is expensed within the group accounts. Additional depreciation = 650,000/5 = $130,000

The machinery is depreciated so the carrying amount at the year-end is $1.62m (1.75m − 0.13 depreciation). Option B is incorrect.

Fair value adjustments are group adjustments and do not create revaluation surpluses. They increase the subsidiary's net assets at acquisition date and consequently goodwill. Option C is incorrect.

The parent's share of extra depreciation required on the fair value adjustment reduces the parent's share of post-acquisition profits held in group retained earnings. Option D is incorrect.

99 D

For group purposes, any contingent liabilities held by the subsidiary will be included within the group accounts at their fair value at acquisition. The contingent liability would reduce the sub's net asset at acquisition and increase goodwill. Option D is correct.

In the individual accounts of the subsidiary contingent liabilities are disclosed but not recognised. However, upon consolidation of the sub, the group will recognise the liability at its fair value at acquisition. Option A is incorrect.

The contingent liability would be updated to its fair value of $110,000 in the consolidated statement of financial position. Therefore, B is incorrect.

The change in the fair value of the contingent liability should be recognised in post-acquisition profit, not as an adjustment to goodwill at acquisition. Therefore, C is incorrect.

100 $85,000

	$000	$000
Consideration paid		1,750
Fair value of NCI		320
Less fair value of net assets at acquisition:		
Share capital	1,000	
Retained earnings	920	
Fair value uplift (745 − 680)	65	
		(1,985)
Goodwill at acquisition and at reporting date		85

ANSWERS TO OBJECTIVE TEST QUESTIONS : SECTION 2

101 B

Non-controlling interest:	$
Fair value of NCI at acquisition	320,000
NCI share of post-acquisition reserves	
20% × 110,250 (see below)	22,050
	342,050

Post-acquisition reserves of ZF:	$
Retained earnings at reporting date	1,100,000
Less retained earnings at acquisition	(920,000)
Fair value depreciation: 65,000/5 × 9/12	(9,750)
Unrealised profit: 300,000 × 20%	(60,000)
	110,250

102 A, D, E

The group share of EMS's post-acquisition earnings will be credited, not debited, to consolidated retained earnings. Therefore, B is incorrect.

The impact that the unrealised profit adjustment has on consolidated retained earnings is $96,000 (80% × $120,000). As the subsidiary made the profit, 20% of the unrealised amount will be deducted from non-controlling interests, with the parent's share being deducted from consolidated retained earnings. Therefore, C is incorrect.

Tutorial note:

The same applies to the fair value depreciation, with 80% of the amount being charged to consolidated retained earnings. Therefore, both D and E are correct.

103 $4,375,000

Property, plant and equipment at 31 December 20X2:	$000
JK	3,300
LM	850
Fair value uplift (1,100,000 − (500,000 + 350,000))	250
Fair value depreciation (250,000 × 1/10)	(25)
	4,375

> **Tutorial note:**
>
> The fair value uplift is calculated by deducting the carrying amount of net assets from the fair value. The fair value is given in the question as $1,100,000 and the carrying amount is the share capital of 500,000 plus the reserves at acquisition of $350,000.

104 B

	$000
Fair value of consideration paid:	
Shares 500,000 × $3.50	1,750
Cash	408
Deferred consideration 1,000,000 × 0.842 (9% discount for 2 years)	842
Legal and professional fees – don't include (should be expensed)	–
	3,000

105 $44,000

	$
Fair value of non-controlling interest at acquisition (20% × 500,000 × $1.80)	180,000
Value of non-controlling interest using proportion of net assets (20% × 680,000)	(136,000)
	44,000

> **Tutorial note:**
>
> The only difference in goodwill between the two methods is the value used for the non-controlling interest at acquisition. Therefore, the above calculation is all that's needed to answer the question. The fair value of NCI is normally given in the question. However, if it is not provided, information regarding the share price must be given. Here the share price was $1.80 at acquisition and this is multiplied by the number of shares owned by the NCI to obtain the fair value of NCI at the acquisition date.

106 B

	$000	$000
Consideration paid		3,250
Fair value of NCI		1,325
Less fair value of net assets at acquisition:		
Share capital	1,000	
Retained earnings	1,500	
Fair value uplift (1,600 – 1,200)	400	
		(2,900)
Goodwill at acquisition		1,675
Less impairment		(425)
Goodwill at the reporting date		1,250

107 C

The fair value adjustment relates to non-depreciable property and will not affect the post-acquisition reserves of DH or the consolidated retained earnings of the BZ group. Therefore, C is incorrect.

As the non-controlling interest is measured at fair value at acquisition, only BZ's share of the impairment will be charged to consolidated retained earnings = 70% × $850,000 = $595,000.

108 C

Non-controlling interest:	$
Fair value of NCI at acquisition	1,325,000
NCI share of post-acquisition reserves	
30% × (2,750,000 – 1,500,000)	375,000
NCI share of goodwill impairment	
30% × 425,000	(127,500)
	1,572,500

109 A

Post-acquisition reserves of FG:	$
Total comprehensive income for the year	125,000
Fair value depreciation	(30,000)
Goodwill impairment	(15,000)
	80,000
Group share	× 65%
	52,000

SUBJECT F2: ADVANCED FINANCIAL REPORTING

> *Tutorial note:*
>
> *As the subsidiary was acquired exactly one year ago, the calculation above is similar to that performed to calculate the NCI share of total comprehensive income for the year. The only difference here is that the group share is calculated rather than the NCI share.*
>
> *If the subsidiary is acquired more than one year ago and the group is calculating the amount that would appear in consolidated reserves, the group would need to include cumulative figures to date. The calculation would start with reserves at the reporting date, deduct reserves at acquisition and then adjust for cumulative consolidation adjustments to date, i.e. depreciation, impairment etc.*

110 A, D, F

Goodwill impairment only affects the non-controlling interest if the fair value method has been used to measure the non-controlling interest at acquisition. Therefore, B is incorrect.

Provisions for unrealised profits only affect the non-controlling interest if the subsidiary made the profit on the transaction. If the parent made the sales, the non-controlling interest is not affected, therefore, C is incorrect.

The non-controlling interest's share of any dividend paid by the subsidiary would be reflected in the consolidated statement of changes in equity. It is the parent's share that would be eliminated upon consolidation. Therefore, E is incorrect.

111 B

NCI share of total comprehensive income:	$
Subsidiary TCI (post-acquisition) = 90,000 × 9/12	67,500
Fair value depreciation	(20,000)
Goodwill impairment	(30,000)
	17,500
NCI share	× 20%
	3,500

> *Tutorial note:*
>
> *The provision for unrealised profit is not included in the above calculation as the parent made the profit and, therefore, the adjustment does not affect the subsidiary's total comprehensive income.*

ANSWERS TO OBJECTIVE TEST QUESTIONS : SECTION 2

112 B, C, D

Any profit on the sale of goods by the parent to the subsidiary would be deducted from the total comprehensive income attributable to the parent shareholders, not the NCI. Therefore, A is incorrect.

The dividend paid by SU is reflected as a distribution of profit rather than part of profit in SU's financial statements. Therefore, its elimination does not affect the NCI calculation and E is incorrect.

113 $720,000

Net assets of TR at reporting date:	$000
Carrying amount	2,500
Fair value uplift	475
Fair value depreciation 475 × 4/20	(95)
	2,880
NCI share	× 25%
NCI at reporting date	720

Tutorial note:

As the NCI is measured using the proportion of net assets method, the NCI at the reporting date will be the NCI share of the net assets at the reporting date, as shown above. An alternative way to calculate this is below. Note that goodwill impairment is not included in the calculation as it is all charged to consolidated reserves when NCI is measured using the proportionate method.

	$000
NCI at acquisition 25% × (1,220 + 475 FV)	423.75
NCI share of post-acquisition reserves 25% × (2,500 – 1,220)	320
NCI share of FV depreciation 25% × (475 × 4/20)	(23.75)
NCI at reporting date	720

114 $8,180,000

Property, plant and equipment at 31 December 20X2:	$000
ER	5,900
MR	2,000
Fair value uplift	400
Fair value depreciation (400,000 × 3/10)	(120)
	8,180

SUBJECT F2: ADVANCED FINANCIAL REPORTING

115 C

NCI share of profit:	$
Subsidiary profit (post-acquisition) = 180,000 × 6/12	90,000
Fair value depreciation	(15,000)
Unrealised profit = 100,000 × 30% × 30%	(9,000)
	66,000
NCI share	× 25%
	16,500

Tutorial note:

The goodwill impairment is not included in the calculation as the non-controlling interest is measured using the proportionate method and, therefore, all impairment is allocated to the profit attributable to parent shareholders.

116 A

Group reserves calculation	$
100% Reserves of Tom	400,000
Tom % of post-acquisition reserves of Jerry	
80% × ($50,000 – $30,000)	16,000
Impairment (W1)	(21,600)
Total reserves at 31 December 20X9	394,400

(W1) Goodwill (for impairment calculation)

	$
Cost of investment	100,000
Reserves at acquisition ($30,000 + $50,000)	(80,000)
NCI (20% × $80,000)	16,000
	36,000
Impairment 60%	(21,600)
Goodwill at 31 December 20X9	14,400

ANSWERS TO OBJECTIVE TEST QUESTIONS : SECTION 2

117 A

	$	%
Revenue	33,000	125
Cost of sales ($33,000/125 × 100)	(26,400)	100
Gross profit ($33,000/125 × 25)	6,600	25
Remaining inventory	50%	
Provision for unrealised profit	3,300	

Inventory and profit are overstated. As a result, inventory is reduced by $3,300 and cost of sales is increased by $3,300.

118 B

PUP Adjustment calculation

	$	%
Revenue	36,000	150
Cost of sales ($36,000/150 × 100)	(24,000)	100
Gross profit ($36,000/150 × 50)	12,000	50

The PUP adjustment of $12,000 is included in the group accounts by reducing group profits (by increasing cost of sales – thus reducing group retained earnings in the SOFP) and reducing inventory.

As the parent sold to the sub, all of the unrealised profit is adjusted in the group profits. NCI does not take any share of the required PUP. If the sub had sold to the parent, the NCI would take a share of the PUP.

The revenue and cost of sales would be reduced by the impact of the intra-group transactions. However, the adjustments required are for the total revenues figures from intra-group trade being $168,000 rather than $36,000.

119 C

The intra-group sales will require a reduction in revenue and cost of sales for the total annual revenue from intra-group trading. $50,000 was sold from the parent to the subsidiary during the period. This amount will be removed from both revenue and cost of sales within the consolidated statement of profit or loss.

As the goods from intra-group trade still remain in the group, a PURP adjustment of $10,000 ($50,000 × 25/125) is required. This is added to group cost of sales.

Revenue of $1,700k (1,000k + 750k – 50k) and cost of sales of $860k (650k + 250k – 50k +10k) are shown in the group statement of profit or loss.

120 C

The intra-group outstanding balances would need to be cancelled out within the group accounts. The cash-in-transit would be recorded before cancellation can arise. As the $5,000 cash is already included within WX's $10,000 payable, an amount of $15,000 must be included in YZ's receivables.

Cash of the group would increase by $5,000, payables reduced by $10,000 and receivables reduced by $15,000.

SUBJECT F2: ADVANCED FINANCIAL REPORTING

121 B

	$	%
Revenue	6,000	133.33
Cost of sales ($6,000/133.33 × 100)	(4,500)	100
Gross profit ($6,000/133.33 × 33.33)	1,500	33.33

The PUP adjustment of $1,500 is included in the group accounts by reducing group profits (by increasing cost of sales) and reducing inventory.

122 C

While having the majority of shares may be a situation which leads to control, it does not feature in the definition of control per IFRS 10 *Consolidated Financial Statements*.

123 C, D

The fair value of deferred consideration is its present value. Fair values are applied to the subsidiary's assets, liabilities and contingent liabilities.

While the use of fair value may initially seem to not comply with the historical cost principle, the fair values of the assets form part of the cost of the subsidiary to the parent, so the principle is still applied. The new fair values are the cost of the sub's net assets to the group.

Depreciation will not increase if the fair value of assets is lower than the current carrying amount or the adjustment is applied to a non-depreciable asset.

124 $2,780,000

The cost of investment is worked out as follows:

Shares: 800,000 × ¾ × $3.80 = $2,280,000

Deferred cash = $550,000 × $1/1.1$ = $500,000

The professional fees cannot be capitalised as part of the cost of investment. Therefore, the total cost of investment is $2,280,000 + $500,000 = **$2,780,000.**

When determining the fair value of the deferred cash using the discount factor of 0.909 from the discount table, the answer of $499,950 would be rounded to $500,000 when working to the nearest $000. This should still give an overall answer of **$2,780**,000 to input.

ASSOCIATES AND JOINT ARRANGEMENTS

125 Arrangement, operation, venture

As per IFRS 11 *Joint arrangements*:

A joint arrangement is an **arrangement** in which two parties or more have joint control. A joint **operation** is where the parties that have joint control have rights to the assets, and obligations for the liabilities, relating to the arrangement. A joint **venture** is where the parties that have joint control have rights to the net assets of the arrangement.

ANSWERS TO OBJECTIVE TEST QUESTIONS : SECTION 2

126 C

The associate has made the sales to the parent, therefore, the unrealised profit should be deducted from the associate's profit and the parent's (and, therefore, group's) inventory.

The unrealised profit is calculated as follows:

	$
Sales value of goods still held: 200,000/2	100,000
Profit on above sales: 100,000 × 25%	25,000
Group share: 25,000 × 35%	8,750

127 B

The dividend would not have been in WeeJoe's statement of profit or loss. Brendan's share would be removed from consolidated investment income as Brendan will have recorded the income in its individual financial statements. The associate's profits are not affected.

The PUP adjustment is calculated as follows:

	$	%
Sales	25,000	125
Cost of sales	(20,000)	100
Gross profit	5,000	25
80% left in Brendan's inventory	4,000	
Unrealised element (P%)	30%	
PUP adjustment	1,200	

The unrealised element of the profit from sales between an associate and a parent is the parent's share of the total profit from goods left in the group.

The profit needs to be time-apportioned for the six months of ownership, with the $15,000 impairment then deducted.

Share of profit of associate = 30% × $300,000 ($600,000 × 6/12) – $1,200 – $15,000 = $73,800

128 B

The investment in associate is calculated as

		$
Cost of investment	[(20% × 1,000,000)/4] × $4.50	225,000
P% × A's post-acquisition movement in net assets	[20% × ($4,600,000 – $5,000,000)]	(80,000)
less		
Impairment		(100,000)
PUP (when P sells to A)		(10,000)
		35,000

Dolph own 20% of Chuck's shares, therefore, Dolph has bought 200,000 shares (20% of Chuck's 1,000,000 shares).

As Dolph issued 1 share for every 4 purchased, Dolph issued 50,000 new shares to acquire Chuck. These had a market value of $4.50 and were worth $225,000.

Dolph must include 20% of Chuck's post-acquisition movement in net assets. Chuck has made a post-acquisition loss of $400,000 (net assets at acquisition were $5,000,000 [share capital $1,000,000 + retained earnings $4,000,000] and net assets at 31 December 20X8 were $4,600,000).

Post-acquisition loss = $4,600,000 − $5,000,000 = $400,000 loss.

The impairment in Chuck of $100,000 must be removed from the value of the investment in the associate.

The PUP adjustment when Dolph (parent) sells to Chuck (associate) is calculated as P% of intra-group profit on goods left in the group = 20% × $50,000 = $10,000. This is removed from the investment in associate when P sells to A.

129 The answer is **$25,900**.

Investment in associate

	$
Cost of investment	25,000
Profits after dividends (6,500 − 3,500) × 30%	900
Investment in associate	25,900

130 B

Impairment of an associate investment of $1,000 will reduce the parent's share of the associate's profit.

131

30% of the share capital of Hansen Co. The other 70% is owned by Lawro, another listed entity, whose directors make up Hansen's board.	Subsidiary
80% of the share capital of Kennedy Co, whose activities are significantly different from the rest of the Nicol group.	Associate
30% of the share capital of Bruce Co. The Nicol group have appointed 2 of the 5 board members of Bruce Co, with the other board members coming from three other entities.	Investment

Normally 30% would suggest that Nicol have significant influence, making Hansen an associate. However, Lawro having 70% and controlling the entire board would mean that it is unlikely that Nicol have influence and, therefore, treat it as a trade investment.

132 **$325,000**

	$
Share of Net Profit: 30% × 1,500,000	450,000
Share of PUP: 30% × ((2m × 50%) × 30%)	(90,000)
Current year impairment	(35,000)
Total	**325,000**

ANSWERS TO OBJECTIVE TEST QUESTIONS : SECTION 2

133 A, B

Items C and D would signify control.

134 $1,335,000

	$000	
Investment at cost	1,200	
Share of post-acquisition profit	150	(750 × $^8/_{12}$ × 30%)
Inventory PUP	(15)	(300 × $^{20}/_{120}$ × 30%)
	1,335	

Tutorial note:

Watch out for the date of acquisition of the associate. The associate was acquired part way through the year!

135

To consolidate an associated investment, the group would **not consolidate** the assets and liabilities of the associate and **would not eliminate** any outstanding intra-group balances between the parent and the associate.

CONSOLIDATED STATEMENT OF CASH FLOWS AND CSOCIE

136 D, E, F

Items A, B and C would all appear within the investing activities section.

137 A, C

Items B, D and E would all appear within the operating activities section.

138 D

Movement in inventory	$000
Balance b/f	36,000
Acquisition of subsidiary	3,600
	39,600
Decrease in inventory (balancing figure)	(4,800)
Balance c/f	34,800

A decrease in inventory is shown as an addition to profit in the operating activities section of the statement of cash flows.

139 $2,200,000

Movement in PPE:	$000
Balance b/f	15,600
Depreciation	(1,800)
Acquisition of subsidiary	800
	14,600
Purchase of PPE (balancing figure = cash paid)	2,200
Balance c/f	16,800

140 C

Movement in NCI:	$000
Balance b/f	18,300
NCI share of total comprehensive income	680
Acquisition of subsidiary 30% × 4,400	1,320
	20,300
Dividends paid to NCI (balancing figure)	(800)
Balance c/f	19,500

141 $2,130,000

Movement in retained earnings:	$000
Balance b/f	20,100
Profit attributable to parent shareholders	3,880
	23,980
Dividends paid to parent shareholders (balancing figure)	(2,130)
Balance c/f	21,850

142 B

Movement in investment in associate:	$000
Balance b/f	5,700
Share of associate's profit for the year	1,800
Share of associate's other comprehensive income for the year	200
	7,700
Dividends received from associate (cash inflow = bal figure)	(1,500)
Balance c/f	6,200

143 A

Movement in goodwill:	$000
Balance b/f	7,200
Acquisition of subsidiary (see below)	1,370
	8,570
Impairment (balancing figure)	(570)
Balance c/f	8,000

Goodwill arising on acquisition of subsidiary:

	$000
Cash consideration	500
Shares consideration 1,000 × 3.95	3,950
Value of NCI 30% × 4,400	1,320
Less fair value of net assets acquired	(4,400)
	1,370

144 C

The parent's share of total comprehensive income (TCI) includes the parent's TCI plus the subsidiary's TCI less NCI share of subsidiary's TCI.

This is calculated as $850,000 (650k + 250k − (20% × 250k).

145 A

The NCI share of total comprehensive income (TCI) is NCI% × subsidiary's TCI. This would be $25,000 (10% × 250k).

The NCI share of dividend paid takes the NCI% × dividend paid by the subsidiary. This would be $10,000 (10% × 100k).

FOREIGN CURRENCY CONSOLIDATIONS

146 B, E

The exchange difference arising on translation of a foreign operation is recognised in other comprehensive income, therefore, A is incorrect.

There is no requirement for subsidiaries to present financial statements in the presentation currency of the parent (although the subsidiaries may choose to do so), therefore, C is incorrect.

The exchange difference on goodwill is only allocated between parent shareholders and non-controlling interest if the non-controlling interest is measured at fair value at the date of acquisition. Therefore, D is incorrect.

147 $9,409

	Crowns
Consideration paid	204,000
Less fair value of net assets at acquisition (1,000 + 180,000)	(181,000)
Goodwill at acquisition	23,000
Less impairment (10%)	(2,300)
Goodwill at the reporting date	20,700

Goodwill at reporting date translated at closing rate = 20,700/2.2 = $9,409

148 C

	A$
NCI share of total comprehensive income:	
Subsidiary's profit translated at average rate = 800,000/2.1	380,952
Exchange loss on net assets	(50,000)
	330,952
NCI share	× 20%
	66,190

The exchange loss on goodwill is fully attributable to the parent shareholders, as non-controlling interest is measured at acquisition using the proportionate method.

149 Exchange difference on net assets for the year:

Exchange difference on net assets		$
Closing net assets at	closing rate	X
Less: comprehensive income at	average rate for the year	(X)
Less: opening net assets at	opening rate	(X)
Exchange difference on net assets for the year		X

ANSWERS TO OBJECTIVE TEST QUESTIONS : SECTION 2

150 $54,000 gain

	Crowns	Exchange rate	
	000		$000
Consideration paid	13,984		
Fair value of NCI	3,496		
Less fair value of net assets acquired	(15,800)		
Goodwill at acquisition	1,680	/ 1.61	1,043
Less impairment (20% × 1,680)	(336)	/ 1.58	(213)
Exchange difference (balancing figure)			54
Goodwill at the reporting date	1,344	/ 1.52	884

Goodwill at the year-end has increased by $54,000 due to exchange rate differences. Therefore, this is a foreign currency gain.

151 C

	Dinar	Exchange rate	
	000		$
Net assets at start of year (3,800 – 1,350)	2,450	/ 36	68,056
Comprehensive income for year	1,350	/ 35	38,571
			106,627
Exchange difference (balancing figure)			12,123
Net assets at reporting date	3,800	/ 32	118,750

152 B

	B$000
Consideration paid (5,200 × 0.50)	2,600
Fair value of NCI	600
Less fair value of net assets acquired	(2,800)
Goodwill at acquisition and reporting date	400

Goodwill at reporting date translated at closing rate = 400,000/0.71 = A$563,380

SUBJECT F2: ADVANCED FINANCIAL REPORTING

153 B

Property, plant and equipment	Gr	$
GD		12,800,000
WR:		
Carrying amount	4,300,000	
Fair value adjustment	500,000	
Fair value depreciation 500 × 3/40	(37,500)	
	4,762,500 /4.1	1,161,585
		13,961,585

154 B, D

A is incorrect. As per IAS 21 *The effects of changes in foreign exchange rates*, the functional currency of NJ is the currency of the primary economic environment in which it operates and is set at individual entity level. Therefore, A is incorrect (and B is correct).

C is incorrect. Sales prices/revenue is only one of the factors to be considered in determining the functional currency and this can be outweighed by other factors, as is the case here. As NJ's costs are incurred in the Kron, it operates autonomously and raises finance in the Kron, the Kron should be its functional currency (therefore D is correct).

The directors of NJ can choose the presentation currency. It does not have to be the functional currency and, therefore, E is incorrect.

INTEGRATED REPORTING

155 An integrated report, external, value

An integrated report is a concise communication about how an organisation's strategy, governance, performance and prospects, in the context of its external environment, lead to the creation of value over the short, medium and long term.

156 B, C, D, E, F

The capitals in the International <IR> Framework are categorised as financial, manufactured, intellectual, human, social and relationship, and natural capital.

157 A, C and F

B – An integrated report may be **either** a standalone report or included as a distinguishable, prominent and accessible part of another report or communication.

D – Although mostly guidance, there are a small number of compulsory requirements for an integrated report to comply with the <IR> Framework.

E – An organisation preparing an integrated report is not required to adopt the categorisation of the capitals in the <IR> Framework (nor to structure the report around the capitals).

ANSWERS TO OBJECTIVE TEST QUESTIONS : SECTION 2

158 A

The dilution of the primary focus of users on financial objectives and towards other non-traditional reporting areas is deemed an advantage of <IR>. It is argued, by placing a greater priority on non-financial implications, <IR> will enable a greater long-term appreciation of the ways that value is created by an entity.

Increased understanding of an entity by most users would be a benefit but for COMPETITORS would be a limitation as the entity may lose competitive advantages.

Increased costs and subjectivity are also limitations.

159 C

As the lake is natural and not man-made, this could be disclosed as a natural capital which creates value for the entity.

ANALYSING FINANCIAL STATEMENTS

160 75.4%

Gearing ratio = debt (W1)/equity = 500/663 × 100 = 75.4%

(W1) Debt:	$m
Long-term borrowings	400
Redeemable preference shares	100
	500

161 17.3 TIMES

Profit before interest and tax (PBIT) = 179 + 11 = $190m

Interest cover = PBIT/finance costs = 190/11 = 17.3 times

162 37.4%

Profit before interest and tax (excluding associate) = 268 − 55 = $213m

Capital employed (excluding associate) = equity + debt − investment in associate

= 465 + 190 − 86 = $569m

Return on capital employed = 213/569 × 100 = 37.4%

SUBJECT F2: ADVANCED FINANCIAL REPORTING

163 C

A is incorrect. A significant investment in PPE shortly before the year end would result in a large increase in capital employed with little effect in profit.

B is incorrect. A revaluation of land and buildings will increase capital employed (revaluation surplus is part of equity) but will have no positive effect on profit.

C is correct. The impact on capital employed would be in the previous period and, therefore, in the current year's ratio the improvement in profitability would be reflected.

D is incorrect. An issue of shares to repay long-term borrowings would have no effect on capital employed (as both equity and debt are included in the calculation). There would be a saving in finance costs, however the profit used in the ROCE calculation does not include finance costs and, therefore, the ratio would not be affected.

164 B, C, D

A is possibly true however the fall in retained earnings could also be caused by a significant dividend payment.

E is possibly true however the increase in long-term borrowings could arise from amortisation of the liability rather than additional borrowings.

165 C

There are various ways that gearing can be calculated, so, to be comparable, firstly the method used for entity B needs to be determined.

Gearing of entity B = 5.9% and equity = 3,403.

Therefore, the figures used for the numerator must be 5.9% × 3,403 = 200.8

Looking at B's figures, it appears that only long-term borrowings have been included in the calculation (200/3,403 = 5.9%)

Therefore, the comparable gearing ratio for A = 1,000/3,754 = 26.6%

166 B

A is incorrect. A's revenue is significantly lower than B's and, therefore, B is more likely to be benefiting from economies of scale.

B is correct, as follows:

	A $m		B $m
Gross profit = 26% × $160m	41.6	Gross profit = 17% × $300m	51
Operating profit = 9% × $160m	14.4	Operating profit = 11% × $300m	33
Operating expenses	27.2		18

C is incorrect. Gross profit margin increases coupled with operating profit margin decreases would suggest that A has high operating expenses. It does not prove any creative accounting or unethical behaviour on behalf of the directors of A.

D is incorrect. LOP's gross profit margin is higher than both A's and B's and, therefore, the acquisition of either entity is likely to reduce the overall margin of the combined business (unless cost savings can be achieved as a result of the acquisition).

ANSWERS TO OBJECTIVE TEST QUESTIONS : SECTION 2

167 A

B is incorrect. VVD has higher gearing than ROB and, therefore, reduced capacity for additional borrowings.

C is incorrect. VVD has higher gearing than ROB and would be considered a higher risk by lenders. The low interest rate may, however, explain why VVD are using debt finance in the first place. The lower interest could suggest financiers see less risk in VVD than ROB but this would be due to other factors outside of the gearing level or VVD's better negotiation skills. The higher gearing of VVD suggests greater risk.

D is incorrect. VVD's lower operating profit margin does not indicate that ROB operates in the budget sector of the market. VVD's higher gross profit margin could suggest that it can charge higher prices than ROB. Its lower operating margin suggests higher operating costs. This could be caused by higher rentals as a result of operating out of more prestigious locations than ROB. It would appear more likely that ROB would be the budget operator.

168 B

Different tax rates would affect any comparison of the profit after tax margin, but has no effect on profit from operations and, therefore, the profit from operations margin.

169 B

Profit margins:	**20X9**		**20X8**	
Gross = 372/1,430	26%	Gross = 317/1,022	31%
Operating = 130/1,430	9%	Operating = 155/1,022	15%

Both gross and operating profit margins have fallen, therefore, A and D are correct.

The increase in distribution costs is 68% compared to an increase in revenue of 40%, therefore, B is incorrect and C is correct.

170 A

A's revenue is similar, and slightly lower, than B's so economies of scale is not a valid explanation of the difference in gross profit margins.

171 B, D, E

A potential minority shareholder would not have access to the information suggested in A or C.

The other information would be readily available.

172 D

An increase in the payables payment period should improve the cash position, as the entity is delaying cash outflows. It may be a consequence of a lack of cash, but not the reason for it.

173 B

A is incorrect as a significant outflow in investing activities suggest growth.

C is incorrect. It is not a certainty that QW has made a profit, it could have significant non-cash items in expenses that, when added back, reconcile a loss to a cash inflow.

D is incorrect as QW still have positive cash and cash equivalents of $590m at the year end.

SUBJECT F2: ADVANCED FINANCIAL REPORTING

174 B

Gearing is calculated as debt/equity or debt/debt + equity. If an item of property plant and equipment is revalued during a period, an increase in revaluation surplus would arise. This is the case for EE.

The increase in revaluation will cause the equity to increase. In turn, the gearing will be expected to reduce.

Gearing 20X1 = 585/1,593 = 36.7%

Gearing 20X2 = 553/1,437 = 38.5%

'EE must have made a loss in the year as retained earnings have fallen' is not true. The fall in retained earnings could also be caused by a significant dividend payment, not necessarily because EE is loss making.

Bonus issues in shares are free issues of shares. They would cause an increase in share capital. No cash is received from these shares. No increase in share premium would arise. As share premium has increased as well as share capital, new shares must have been issued during the year for cash in excess of the nominal value of the shares.

'EE must have secured additional long-term borrowings of $25m' is not necessarily true. The increase in long-term borrowings could arise from amortisation of the liability rather than additional borrowings.

175 C, E

The following statements are not realistic expectations:

'VB has recorded significant gains on the change in fair value of its FVOCI investments' is not a realistic explanation as this would decrease gearing. There would be an increase in VB's equity caused by an increase in the FVOCI reserve. VB would be expected to have a lower gearing than JK.

'VB's management is better at controlling costs than JK's' is not a valid explanation. VB would be expected to have higher profits, thus higher retained earnings in equity and lower gearing.

'VB has reduced its effective tax rate by employing tax accountants' is not a realistic explanation. The fees for the tax accountants and the tax benefit are held in profits. This would increase VB's profits in comparison to JK (assuming the benefits of using the accountant outweigh the costs). This would increase retained earnings in equity causing a reduction to gearing.

176 A, D, E

B is incorrect. The gross profit margin for retail operations in 20X2 is 30.0% (1,200/4,004) compared with 29.6% (1,095/3,700) last year.

C is incorrect. The shop overheads would affect operating profit and profit before tax margins, but not the gross profit margin.

F is incorrect. The online store has a higher profit before tax margin (138/1,096 = 12.6%) than the hotel contract (82/900 = 9.1%).

ANSWERS TO OBJECTIVE TEST QUESTIONS : **SECTION 2**

177 0.4 TIMES

Dividend cover = Profit for the year/Dividend paid

$750,000/(3,750,000 × 0.5) = $750,000/1,875,000

178 A, B, E

Non-current asset turnover = Revenue/NCAs.

C is incorrect. A revaluation of non-current assets would reduce non-current asset turnover and, therefore, result in A's being lower than B's.

D is incorrect. A manufacturing entity would have a higher level of NCAs and, therefore, a lower NCA turnover than a service entity.

179 Formula for dividend cover:

Dividend cover
Net profit for the year
Dividend paid during the year

180 C

Interest cover is not affected as no time has elapsed during 20X6 for the finance costs to accrue. C is incorrect.

Current ratio considers current assets vs current liabilities. Acquisitions of plant and machinery and bank loans are considered non-current assets and liabilities. Current ratio is not impacted by the transaction.

Gearing would be expected to increase as a result of the higher levels of debt.

ROCE would be expected to reduce as operating profits would be unaffected and capital employed would increase. No time exists during the year ended March 20X6 for any discernible benefit to arise from the investment in the PPE. It would be reasonable to assume that profits are unaffected. The capital employed would increase as a result of the new long-term financing.

181 A, C, D

Profit is not affected as the land is non-depreciable and the revaluation surplus would be credited to other comprehensive income rather than profit. Therefore, B is incorrect.

The current ratio only includes current assets (and liabilities) and, therefore, E is incorrect.

182 D

A is not valid. The increase in the long-term borrowings is more likely to be from amortising the liability element of the convertible bonds rather than raising additional finance. Either way, the small increase in liabilities would not be enough to reduce the ROCE when coupled with the increase in profit margins.

B is not valid. Increased finance costs would not be reflected in the return on capital employed as the profit used in the calculation is before deduction of finance costs.

C is not valid. Both gross profit margin and profit before tax margin have increased, therefore, it would be highly unlikely (although not impossible!) that the operating margin would have fallen.

SUBJECT F2: ADVANCED FINANCIAL REPORTING

183 1.54

Asset turnover = Revenue/capital employed

Asset turnover = 4,800/3,116 (W1) = 1.54

(W1) Capital employed = equity + long term and short term borrowings = 2,600 + 400 + 116 = 3,116

184 A

A is not a limitation when comparing a single entity from one period to the next. If an entity changes an accounting policy it is required to restate its comparatives to reflect the new policy and, therefore, comparison will still be made on a like for like basis.

Tutorial note:

This would be a limitation when comparing ratios of two different entities.

185 D

Return on capital employed (ROCE) can be calculated either with or without the associate, as long as the numerator and denominator are consistent.

Therefore, firstly consider which method has been used for the calculation of B's ROCE.

With associate included, B's ROCE = (509 + 32)/(1,500 + 650) = 25.2%

With associate excluded, B's ROCE = (509 + 32 – 25)/(1,500 + 650 – 350) = 28.7%

Therefore, the comparable ROCE for A would exclude the associate.

Comparable ROCE for A = (680 + 25 – 148)/(950 + 500 – 570) = 63.3%

186 a reduction, a reduction, an increase

When assessing reasons for changes in cash and cash equivalents **a reduction** in inventory, **a reduction** in receivables and **an increase** in payables would all explain an improvement in the cash position.

187 A, B, F

LW are unlikely to have increased selling prices when there has been no growth in sales volume for the past five years, therefore, C is not a realistic conclusion.

An increase in payables payment period would improve rather than worsen the cash position, therefore, D is not a realistic conclusion.

The quick ratio does not include inventory and therefore E is not a realistic conclusion.

ANSWERS TO OBJECTIVE TEST QUESTIONS : SECTION 2

188 A, B

Breakdown of operating expenses and cash flow forecasts are internal information and, therefore, would not be readily available.

Industry statistics are available for most industries.

Interim financial statements and operating and financial reviews are typically published by listed entities.

> *Tutorial note:*
>
> *BR could approach the directors of WL to try and access the internal information. In practice, how likely this is to be successful would depend on whether WL are keen for BR to acquire the entity.*

189

Return on capital employed	Gross profit margin
Revenue – cost of sales – operating expenses	Revenue – cost of sales
―――――――――――	―――――――――――
Capital employed	Revenue

190 B

Dividend cover = Profit for the year/Dividend paid

Dividend cover would not be distorted by any incomparability of share prices.

191 B, C, D

A, E and F are all examples of information not typically published by listed entities. It would be highly unlikely that a minority shareholder would be able to obtain copies of these.

192 C

C suggests that X's cost of sales would be relatively higher than Y and this would result in X's gross profit margin being lower rather than higher.

193 B

A revaluation policy would reduce gearing rather than increase it.

194 MORE, X, Y

If further debt finance was required by the new companies, debt finance would be **more** likely to be obtained for Y.

Based upon the gearing levels of the two entities, an investment in **X** would appear to be riskier than an investment in **Y**.

SUBJECT F2: ADVANCED FINANCIAL REPORTING

195 A, C

Although the current and quick ratios have both reduced, they are still at very comfortable levels and, therefore, liquidity is not a significant concern.

Inventory is not included in the quick ratio and, therefore, would not be the reason for a change in it.

Tutorial note:

Over-trading occurs when there is significant growth and a failure to support the growth with long-term finance. It will typically result in an increase in working capital ratios and a reduction in operating cash flows.

196 B

The increase in equity and capital employed would result in a reduction of both ratios.

197 A, B, C, D, E, F

All information is likely to be accessible, as the lender can simply turn down the application for finance if the entity does not provide it.

198 Higher, despite

A is incurring significantly **higher** operating expenses than B. Its return on capital employed is higher than B's **despite** the revaluation of non-current assets in the year.

A revaluation will have a negative effect on ROCE. The operating expenses can actually be calculated from the information provided (although this would not be necessary to answer the question) as follows:

	A $000		B $000
Gross profit = 36% × $5.7m	2,052	Gross profit = 31% × $5.3m	1,643
Operating expenses (bal fig)	(1,396)	Operating expenses (bal fig)	(901)
PBIT = 11.5% × $5.7m	656	PBIT = 14% × $5.3m	742

199 D

D is incorrect.

A has a lower level of debt but a higher finance cost. This would suggest that either A has repaid borrowings part way through the year (its average borrowings are higher than at the year-end) or B has increased its borrowings during the year (and its finance costs, therefore, do not reflect a full year's worth of interest).

ANSWERS TO OBJECTIVE TEST QUESTIONS : SECTION 2

200 B, C, E, F

A is comparable, as the costs of depreciating the computer equipment and the finance costs on the debt for A Ltd and the rental expenses for the short term lease of B Ltd would be charged through administrative expenses. This would leave gross profit margins unaffected.

D is comparable as the current ratio reflects working capital balances and would not be directly affected by the method of finance used for the acquisitions.

The other ratios are all affected by debt or finance costs. A Ltd buys the assets with debt finance, whilst B Ltd finances the computer equipment through low value leases which do not create a lease liability. The ratios which use finance costs and debt are deemed distorted for direct comparison.

201 B

A is not a valid conclusion. The fall in retained earnings could also have been due to a significant dividend payment.

C is not a valid conclusion. The reduction in share premium matches the increase in share capital, suggesting that the issue of shares was a bonus issue which does not raise finance.

D is not a valid conclusion. The increase in borrowings could be amortisation of the existing borrowings rather than additional borrowings being taken out.

202 Investing, financing

When analysing a statement of cash flows, a cash outflow from **investing** activities would suggest that the entity is expanding its operations.

An outflow from investing activities is often matched with an inflow from **financing** activities as long term finance should be used to finance investment.

203 A reduction in selling prices

Given the circumstances that TYU finds itself in, the most likely reason for the reduction in gross profit margin is **a reduction in selling prices**.

This would be the most obvious response to the new entrant to maintain or regain market share. Revenue has not fallen which suggests that this has been a successful move.

204 C

A is not a valid conclusion. An increase in inventory holding period would increase the current ratio (as inventory would be higher).

B is not a valid conclusion. Inventory is excluded from the quick ratio calculation.

D is not a valid conclusion. An increase in inventory at the reporting date would reduce cost of sales (as closing inventory is deducted from this figure) and, therefore, increase the gross profit margin.

SUBJECT F2: ADVANCED FINANCIAL REPORTING

205 A

Although the current ratio is greater than 1, the quick ratio is only 0.5 and, therefore, UYT is facing significant liquidity concerns. The inventory is not a liquid asset, therefore, the quick ratio provides a better measure of liquidity than the current ratio.

The current ratio is likely to only be greater than 1 because of a significant inventory holding.

206 A, B, D, E, F

The measurement of non-controlling interest only affects the calculation of goodwill and the NCI share of equity. Any goodwill impairment would be charged to operating expenses rather than cost of sales so there would be no effect on gross profit.

All of the other differences could affect the calculation of gross profit.

A revaluation of non-current assets will affect the amount of depreciation being charged to profit or loss. If the assets are production related, then depreciation should be charged through cost of sales.

207 C

EBITDA represents earnings before interest, tax, depreciation and amortisation. Earnings is calculated as earnings attributable to ordinary shareholders = PAT – NCI share of profit – irredeemable preference dividends. As no tax is given in the information, earnings can be approximated to be profit before tax (PBT).

	$000
PBT	224
Add back	
Finance cost	15
Depreciation (15 + 5)	20
Amortisation	12
EBITDA	271

The fuel costs and staff salaries are normal operating expenses that should be included as an expense within earnings.

208 C

The Gartner Data Analytics Maturity model identifies 4 stages within data analytics. They are descriptive, diagnostic, predictive and prescriptive.

ANSWERS TO OBJECTIVE TEST QUESTIONS : SECTION 2

RANDOM QUESTION TESTS

RANDOM QUESTION TEST 1

1.1 C

The patent has been acquired and is not internally generated (despite the product itself being internally invented and developed), therefore, should be capitalised and amortised over its lifetime (20 years).

The customer list is an internally generated intangible asset and not recorded within the financial statements.

1.2 B

The bonds are a financial liability as they contain an obligation to pay interest at the coupon rate of 5% and to repay at a premium of 10% after five years.

The bonds are not a financial asset. The bonds have been issued. This means the business is selling the bonds to raise finance. A financial liability is created.

The initial recognition would be at a value of $2,975,000 ($3m less the issue costs of $25,000).

In addition to the coupon payments of 5% each year, there are additional finance costs: the issue costs and the redemption premium. The effective rate of interest will, therefore, be greater than 5%.

The liability is shown at amortised cost over the five years and the carrying amount of the bond will change at each reporting date. The carrying amount is given as:

B/f	Interest at effective interest rate	Payment at coupon rate	C/f
X	X	(X)	X

After 5 years the carrying amount should be $3,300,000 as this is the amount due for repayment on the redemption date. At each year end, however, the amortised cost will be a different value (lower than the $3,300,000).

1.3 26%

$k_d = i(1-T)/P_o$

$(k_d \times P_o)/i = 1-T$

$T = 1 - ((k_d \times P_o)/i)$

$T = 1 - [(0.0976 \times 91)/12]$

$T = 26\%$

SUBJECT F2: ADVANCED FINANCIAL REPORTING

1.4 A

NCI % × S's PAT = 20% × $600k	$120k
NCI% × PURP (S selling to P) = 20% × 60k	($12k)
NCI% × Impairment (NCI at FV) = 20% × $50k	($10k)
Total NCI = $120k – $12k – $10k	**$98k**

1.5 B

The quick ratio is made up of the current assets excluding inventory divided by the current liabilities. In the case of Couts Ltd, this will be receivables and cash divided by payables and the overdraft.

($120,000 + $15,000)/($105,000+$51,000) = 0.87:1.

1.6 B

A new share issue would increase the level of equity. This would, therefore, decrease the level of gearing.

Revaluation losses would either reduce revaluation surplus (if the asset had been previously revalued upwards) or profits. Either way, equity would reduce (any impact to profits would reduce retained earnings). Consequently, gearing would increase.

New loans increase debt and, therefore, gearing.

Assets purchased through bond finance during the year would increase non-current assets and financial liabilities. Hence, gearing would increase.

1.7 A, D

EMI group consists of a 75% sub, LI, which is consolidated from 31 July 20X9.

Therefore, the date of control for LI is 31 July 20X9, not 31 December 20X8. Goodwill will include the fair value of the net assets of LI as at 31 July 20X9, not the 31 December 20X8. Option B is not correct.

EMI has paid for LI using deferred consideration. For cash paid in the future, this would be recorded at the present value of the cash paid. The $10m paid in one year's time is discounted to its present value within the goodwill calculation. Option C is incorrect.

As the sub, LI, is 75% owned by the parent, EMI, 75% of the post-acquisition profits of LI are taken to group retained earnings. Option D is correct.

Consolidation of profit or loss will only occur from the date of acquisition. For LI, being acquired on 31 July 20X9 means that only 5 months of (not the entire years') income and expenses will be 100% consolidated within the EMI group financial statements.

1.8 B

Total revenue = 65% × $12m = $7.8m.

The amount to be recorded in year 2 will be $7.8m less the amounts recorded in year 1.

Revenue recorded in year 2 = 7.8m – 3.25m = $4.55m.

ANSWERS TO OBJECTIVE TEST QUESTIONS : SECTION 2

1.9 D

Intra-group outstanding balances must be eliminated from consolidation. Elimination will only occur once the outstanding balances (payables and receivables) agree.

In this case, the sub (RAT) has despatched goods to the parent (SHA) prior to the year-end, which have not been received by the parent. The goods are in transit at the year end.

Before elimination of the intra-group outstanding balances can occur, the goods in transit must be recorded as if they were delivered before the year end.

Dr Inventory $2.5m Cr Payables $2.5m.

SHA had $45m owing to RAT before this transaction was recorded. Therefore, $47.5m is now shown as outstanding to RAT after the effects of the above entry. Assuming no other items are in transit, this means that RAT must have a receivable of $47.5m.

To eliminate the intragroup outstanding, Dr Payables $47.5m Cr Receivables $47.5m.

The overall result is:

Dr Inventory $2.5m (increasing inventory)

Dr Payables $45m (decreasing payables)

Cr Receivables $47.5m (decreasing receivables)

1.10 A, C, F

Option B states that Y is paying their suppliers on time. Y is actually paying its suppliers earlier than is required, which means it is not maximising the advantages of this cheap source of finance. This could be beneficial if it is taking advantage of settlement discounts. There are no settlement discounts available. Therefore, Y would be better served taking further advantage of the credit available from their suppliers.

Z should not exceed the payment terms offered to it by suppliers. As such, it is not being managed in the best manner. If Z's suppliers do not get paid on time, the suppliers may not deliver raw materials when needed. This would interrupt Z's production and may lead to stock-outs. The supplier could even force Z into liquidation if the failure to pay what is owed continues.

It is impossible to conclude as to whether Y requires a bank overdraft from the information provided.

RANDOM QUESTION TEST 2

2.1 C

Deferred tax arises due to temporary differences between the carrying amount and the tax base. The carrying amount of the provision is a $1m liability. This causes the carrying amount to be lower than the tax base. This will create a deferred tax asset within the financial statements. Suarez will get tax relief when paying the costs associated with the damages. This tax relief creates a deferred tax asset.

Therefore, to record an increase in a deferred tax asset, a debit will be posted to the deferred tax asset/liability account.

The deferred tax ASSET, not liability will have a value of $1m × 25% = $250k as at the year ended 31 December 20X5. A is incorrect.

The movement in the deferred tax asset is $125,000 (DT asset at y/e 31 December 20X5 – DT asset at y/e 31 December 20X4 = [$1m × 25%] – [500k × 25%] = $250k – $125k = $125k). This movement is taken to profit or loss NOT reserves. This is to ensure the tax impact is matched against the accounting treatment of the provision. B is incorrect.

The temporary difference is calculated as the carrying amount – tax base = $1m – 0 = $1m. The tax base of a liability is given as carrying amount – amounts written off in future tax computations.

For y/e 20X5, the carrying amount is $1m, the tax base = 0 ($1m – $1m). The temporary difference is $1m, not $500k. D is incorrect.

2.2 B

The correct statement is 'Upon liquidation of a company, the shareholders will receive a pay-out after all other finance providers have been paid'. Ordinary shareholders are subordinate to all other finance providers so they will receive their pay-out last.

Dividends are paid at the discretion of the directors.

Dividends are a distribution of earnings and paid out of post-tax profits. Dividends paid are represented in the financial statements through retained earnings, rather than in the profit or loss account.

The ordinary shareholders have voting rights.

2.3 A

To calculate basic earnings per share, the weighted average number of shares must be calculated as shown below.

Date	Number	Fraction of year	Weighted Average
1 January	4,000,000	3/12	1,000,000
1 April	5,000,000	9/12	3,750,000
			4,750,000

Basic EPS = $3,400,000/4,750,000 = **$0.72**

ANSWERS TO OBJECTIVE TEST QUESTIONS : SECTION 2

Diluted EPS calculates the interest saved, net of tax, and adds that to the earnings figure. The number of additional shares to be issued is calculated by working out the maximum shares that could be issued. In this case, the maximum number of shares that can be received is if the shareholders convert the loan into 40 shares for every $100.

To work out any interest saved, the carrying amount, not the par value, should be used. The carrying amount of the liability element is $2m. Also the effective interest rate, not the coupon rate, is used. The effective interest rate is 8%.

Additional earnings = Interest saved – additional tax.

Interest saved = $2m × 8% = $160,000

Additional tax = $160,000 × 26% = $41,600.

Additional earnings = (160,000 – 41,600) = $118,400

Additional shares = $2.5million × 40/100 = $1m new shares.

Diluted EPS = ($3,400,000 + $118,400)/ (4,750,000 + 1,000,000) = 61.2 cents

2.4 A

While the website is new in the year, the additional delivery costs are likely to be incurred every year in the future, meaning it is not a 'one-off' item.

2.5 C

No non-controlling interest is shown for associates (as no 100% consolidation occurs). As the subsidiary, DP, was 100% owned, no NCI is shown for the subsidiary either.

SJ only prepares group accounts from the point it controls another entity. This would be from the date SJ acquired DP (1 January 20X5) not from when it acquired the associate, JB. Option A is incorrect.

JB would be treated as an equity financial asset before consolidation. This would be valued to fair value at each reporting date (either as a FVOCI or FVPL financial asset). Only upon acquisition of DP does SJ start consolidating. SJ will include JB as an associate within the group accounts. The investment in associate will include the fair value of the financial asset as at 1 January 20X5 within the investment in associate calculation rather than the original cost of £937,500. Option B is incorrect.

Associates apply equity accounting. The assets and liabilities and income and expenses are not 100% consolidated. Instead the investment in associate is included in the statement of financial position.

2.6 D, E

The supplier payments should be considered as revenue under IFRS 15. The payments are in return for providing advantageous shelf space and offering discounted deals on supplier products. Therefore, there are 2 performance obligations for which revenue must be recorded. This contract provides the suppliers with a service rather than transferring goods. The supplier will receive and consume benefit simultaneously, resulting in the need to recognise revenue over time.

Therefore, revenue is not recognised in advance, as per the policy of Bellamy Ltd, because control is not transferred (control must be transferred for revenue to be recorded at a point in time).

SUBJECT F2: ADVANCED FINANCIAL REPORTING

When revenue is recorded over time, the stage of completion of the contract is used to determine the level of revenue recorded. As the discounted offers and the advantageous shelf space are provided over the 12months, a proportion of the total revenue should be recorded.

The Finance Director may be trying to deliberately overstate revenue by recording the payments in advance. The Finance Director (FD) could be trying to hit bonus targets and misstate the financial statements. Even if the FD was unaware of the stipulations of IFRS 15 for this payment, a person in this important role should investigate the opinions of the Financial Controller to determine the appropriate course of action. The FD does not investigate and sticks with the status quo. This is unethical. The Financial Controller would be within their rights to contact the CIMA ethics helpline.

Bellamy provides a service for a fee where the benefits are simultaneously received and consumed. Revenue should be recorded over time. No goods are sold or provided to the supplier. Risk and rewards transfer is a factor that indicate transfer of control to the customer and is considered when revenue is recorded at a point in time. Revenue relating to Bellamy's service to their suppliers is recognised over time so option C is not applicable.

The Financial Controller (FC) will follow the orders of the FD unless those orders are in direct conflict with the regulatory environment that the professional operates in. The FC will be applying IAS's in their day to day role and should comply with the ethical guidelines of their chosen profession. Accountants have strict ethical guidelines to comply with. The FC would not be following that guidance if they followed orders that they deemed to be unethical.

2.7 B

Operating margin = Profit from operations/revenue = $120,000/$975,000 = **12.3%**

Revenue	$975,000
Cost of sales	($555,000)
Gross profit	$420,000
Operating expenses	($300,000)
Operating profit	$120,000

Dividends received are held under investment income which would be below operating profit.

Dividends paid are accounted for within retained earnings and not the profit or loss account. They do not impact operating profits.

Finance costs and interest received (within investment income) are below operating profits within the profit or loss account.

As a result, dividends received, dividends paid and finance costs are irrelevant for the calculation of operating profit margins.

2.8 B

Growth rate is given via g = r × b

r = return = 8%

b = proportion of profits retained = (1.8m – 0.6m)/1.8m = 66.7%

g = 8% × 66.7% = 5.3%

2.9 A

Parent's share of profits	$000
100% P's (KR's) profit	9,500
P's % of S's (AP's) profit for the year	720
75% × (3,000k – 2,040k)	
	10,220

Non-controlling interest share of profit

NCI share of S's profit for the year	240
25% × (3,000k – 2,040k)	

2.10 E

The cash flow related to NCI that should be shown in the consolidated statement of cash flows for the year ended 31 December 20X8 is $187,500:

Non-controlling interests			
		Brought forward	525,000
Dividends paid to NCI shareholders β	187,500	Total comprehensive income	201,000
Carried forward	603,000	Added on acquisition of the subsidiary	64,500
	790,500		790,500

Dividends paid to NCI are treated as financing activity cash flows. Dividends paid are outflows.

SUBJECT F2: ADVANCED FINANCIAL REPORTING

RANDOM QUESTION TEST 3

3.1 More, higher, shorter

H is **more** liquid than C due to **higher** levels of current assets compared to current liabilities. C's liquidity could be improved if C could make its receivable days **shorter**.

Explanation:

H's current and quick ratios are higher than C's which indicates that H is more liquid than C and has greater current assets compared to current liabilities.

C's receivable days are higher than H's. If C received cash from customers earlier, liquidity would improve and receivable days would be shorter.

3.2 D

The higher of the:

(i) cash paid at redemption or,

(ii) the share price converted at redemption date

is used to work out the 'cash flow' on redemption in an IRR calculation for a convertible bond.

Cash option = 100 × 1.1 = $110

Shares option = 12 × ($8.50 × 1.04^3) = $114.74 = $115

Assume that investor will always choose the higher value option so $115 is the cash flow on redemption.

3.3 D

Annual foreign currency gain or loss on translation can be calculated by:

		$
Closing NA's at closing rate (CR)	3,000,000/20	150,000
less		
Opening NA's @ opening rate (OR)	(3,000,000 – 812,500)= 2,187,500/25	(87,500)
Comprehensive income at average rate (AR)	812,500/22	(36,932)
Forex gain on translation of NA's		**25,568**

3.4 C

Liabilities are initially recorded at their fair value. The fair value for a financial liability is the net proceeds (the nominal value less any issue costs).

Therefore, the initial liability is $45,000 – $750 = $44,250.

The finance cost in the profit or loss account is based on the effective interest rate.

Therefore, the finance charge in the statement of profit or loss will be $3,761 (= $44,250 × 8.5%).

ANSWERS TO OBJECTIVE TEST QUESTIONS : SECTION 2

3.5 B

Moose has entered into a lease with a customer. Moose is the lessor. Moose should firstly determine if the lease is a finance lease or an operating lease. In this case, the lease is a finance lease as the lease term is the majority of the useful life of the asset (lease term = 5 years and useful life is 6 years) and the present value of minimum lease payments is significantly all of the fair value.

On initial recognition of a finance lease, the leased asset is derecognised and a lease receivable is recorded. A gain or loss on disposal is recorded in the statement of profit or loss. The lease receivable is recorded at the present value of minimum lease payments not yet made (also known as the net investment in the lease) = $87,000. The carrying amount on the inception of the lease = $70,000. A gain on disposal of $17,000 is recorded.

Dr Receivable $87,000

Cr Asset $70,000

Cr Profit or loss $17,000

By the reporting date, interest will increase the receivable at the rate implicit with the lease of 4.8%. Lease payments will reduce the receivable.

	b/f	Finance cost at implicit rate associated with lease (4.8%)	Lease rental	c/f
20X6	87,000	4,176	(20,000)	71,176
20X7	71,176	3,416	(20,000)	54,592

The current receivable at the year-end 20X6 will be the total receivable at 31 December 20X6 ($71,176) less the total receivable after the rental payments in the next year, 20X7 ($54,592).

Current receivable = 71,176 – 54,592 = $16,584.

Non-current receivable = $54,592.

3.6 C

The total dividends to be included in the consolidated statement of changes in equity are:

	$
100% of LI's (P) dividend paid	1,800,000
Non-controlling interests share of VE's (Subs) dividend paid (20% × 720,000)	144,000
	1,944,000

RP is an associate. Dividends paid by an associate are not separately included within the group CSOCIE. The parent's (LI) share of the dividend paid by the associate (RP) is cancelled out of the group profit or loss and, instead, the parent's share of the associate's profit after tax (which includes the dividend received from the associate) is included upon equity accounting of the associate. This affects the parent's share of total comprehensive income and not the dividend paid within the CSOCIE.

3.7 D

Inventory days give the average time it takes to sell inventory. If inventory selling prices are reduced, it would be a reasonable expectation that the time it took to sell inventory would decrease. It would be expected that more sales of the inventory lines would occur.

Inventory obsolescence and a slowdown in trading suggest that the entity would struggle to sell the inventory lines. Thus inventory days would increase.

A change in supplier could cause changes to **payable** days as credit terms may change. However, inventory days would not be expected to be directly impacted.

3.8 B, D

Key management personnel of a company are deemed to be related parties of the entity. The chief executive officer would meet this definition and is a related party.

Entities controlled by close family members of key management personnel are also deemed to be related parties. AR, the entity controlled by the chief executive officer's wife is deemed a related party.

Key customers, banks and joint venturers who share joint control in a joint venture are specifically identified by IAS 24 *Related party disclosures* as NOT being related parties to an entity.

3.9 C

WACC is weighted based on market values, not nominal values.

	Market value	Cost	Weight × Cost	Weighted average
Equity	$15 million	13.2%	15/32.5 × 13.2%	6.1%
Irredeemable debt	$7.5 million	8.4%	7.5/32.5 × 8.4%	1.9%
Redeemable debt	$10 million	9.6%	10/32.5 × 9.6%	3.0%
Total	$32.5 million			11.0%

3.10 C

Goodwill in LP:	$
Consideration paid for in cash	5,625,000
Fair value of contingent consideration	1,387,500
	7,012,500
Fair value of NCI at acquisition	1,800,000
Less fair value of net assets acquired	(3,750,000)
	5,062,500

ANSWERS TO OBJECTIVE TEST QUESTIONS : SECTION 2

RANDOM QUESTION TEST 4

4.1 A

Due to the extra competition within the market sector, it would be a reasonable strategy for SH to combat the competition by reducing its sales prices. If SH did lower sales prices gross profit margin would be expected to reduce.

An increase in cost prices would also cause gross profit margins to decrease. However, there are no indications within the scenario that suggest that cost prices would increase.

On this basis, whilst A & C would both contribute to gross profit margin reductions, a decrease in sales price is the most likely contributing factor. Option C (cost price increases) is not as valid an option as option A (reduction in sales prices).

Gross profit margin gives the % gross profit per sale. Gross profit is affected by changes in sales prices, cost prices, inefficiencies and changes in sales mix. Gross profit margins are never impacted simply through changes in volumes of sales or purchases. For volumes to impact gross profit margins, discounts on price would have to be offered in conjunction with the increase in sales volumes. Therefore, reductions in sales volumes only will not reduce GP%. Also, it can be noted that SH's sales have gone up. Option B would not be a valid conclusion.

Finance costs are included below operating profits. Gross profit margins only consider gross profits. Finance costs do not impact gross profit. Option D is not valid.

4.2 C

Despite facing more competition, HS's revenue has still increased. An increase in revenue would reasonably be expected to cause reductions in the inventory holding period (the time it takes to sell inventory on average).

The time it takes to sell inventory should not impact directly on the time it takes to repay the suppliers of HS. It could be argued that a reduction in the time it takes to sell inventory will lead to quicker eventual receipt of the cash from the customers. This could enable payables to be paid off quicker. This would cause a decrease in the payable payment period, not an increase. Option A is incorrect.

Quick ratio is calculated as (current assets − inventory)/current liabilities. Inventory is not included within the calculation. Quick ratio is unaffected by inventory movements. Option B is incorrect.

A decrease in inventory holding period would be expected to cause a reduction in closing stock. Reductions in closing stock would see an increase in cost of sales. As such, option D is incorrect.

4.3 A

Group retained earnings as at 31 January 20X9

	$000
100% of P	10,800
Plus P% of subsidiary's post-acquisition movement in net assets (75% × 1,600(W1))	1,200
Plus P% of associate's post-acquisition movement in net assets (30% × -950(W2))	(285)
Impairment in OB (associate)	(500)
Groups retained earnings at 31 January 20X9	**11,215**

(W1) Net assets of VI

	At reporting date	At acquisition date	Post-acquisition
	$000	$000	$000
Share capital	1,000	1,000	–
Retained earnings	5,250	3,650	1,600
Fair value adjustment – non-depreciable land	450	450	
	6,700	5,100	1,600

(W2) Net assets of OB

	At reporting date	At acquisition date	Post-acquisition
	$000	$000	$000
Share capital	2,000	2,000	–
Retained earnings	3,250	4,200	(950)
	5,250	6,200	(950)

4.4 C

NB. This question requires the cum div share price. That is the share price **before** the dividend payment.

ke with dividend growth =

$$k_e = \frac{d_0 \times (1+g)}{P_0} + g$$

$$P_0 = \frac{d_0 \times (1+g)}{k_e - g}$$

$$P_0 = \frac{0.5 \times 1.07}{0.149 - 0.07} = 6.77$$

Ex div price = $6.77

Cum div price = $6.77 + $0.50

Cum div price = $7.27

4.5 A

	$000
Parent dividend paid – 100% P	1,000
Dividend paid to non-controlling interest	
NCI % × S's dividend paid	250
25% × $1,000k	

ANSWERS TO OBJECTIVE TEST QUESTIONS : SECTION 2

4.6 D

CD has made an investment in bonds that would be treated as a financial asset.

The asset would be classified and measured at amortised cost. The bonds are debt financial assets and CD has the intention to hold them until the maturity date. This is consistent with CD's overall business model for similar financial assets.

The transaction costs of $12,800 (0.5% × $2,560,000) would be added to the asset at initial recognition (NB. Both the $2,560,000 and $12,800 are outflows of cash).

The transaction costs would only be treated as an expense if the asset was classified as FVPL.

4.7 F

The sale is recorded using the historic rate as at 1 October 20X1. This is translated at the exchange rate of 400,000/1.65 = $242,424. Dr Receivable 242,424 Cr Revenue 242,424.

The payment is recorded at the exchange rate when the cash was received of 400,000/1.91 = $209,424. This is to settle the receivable of $242,424. Therefore, a foreign currency **loss** on translation of $33,000 is taken to profit or loss.

Dr Cash 209,424

Dr P/L 33,000

Cr Receivable 242,424

4.8 B

The cost of investment is included at the fair value of consideration.

The fair value of shares issued as consideration is the market value at the acquisition date. The market value of HI's shares issued at 30 June 20X4 was $3.80.

Shares in HI: 800,000 × ¾ × $3.80 = $2,280,000

The fair value of deferred cash is the present value of the payments.

Deferred cash = $550,055 × 0.909 = $500,000

The professional fees cannot be capitalised as part of the cost of investment. Therefore, the total fair value of the consideration is $2,280,000 + $500,000 = **$2,780,000**

4.9 B, D

The share price is only one way of measuring a company's value. Its market capitalisation (share price multiplied by number of shares) is widely used by investment analysts but there is no 'exact' measure of a company's value.

A stock market flotation is expensive and time consuming due to, for example, advisor fees and legal fees.

The original owners must dilute their shareholding by making shares available for the public to buy on the flotation.

4.10 D

Option A is incorrect. It is accurate so far as to say that impairment is not a cash flow – it is an expense. However, the impairment expense will cause an adjustment to the reconciliation from profit before tax to cash generated from operations. The impairment does affect the cash flow statement.

Option B is incorrect. The NET cash outflow from acquiring a subsidiary is included in 'cash flows from investing activities', not the GROSS cash flow. The net cash flow includes the gross amount paid to acquire the subsidiary less the cash held by the sub at acquisition (that is 100% consolidated as part of the CSOFP).

Option C is incorrect. The dividend received from associates is an actual cash inflow for the group and is included within 'cash flows from investing activities'. The parent's share of associate's profits will be adjusted as part of the reconciliation to calculate 'cash generated from operations', not the dividend received.

RANDOM QUESTION TEST 5

5.1 B

Goodwill of IVY as at 31 January 20X9

	$000
Consideration paid	5,000
Fair value of non-controlling interest at acquisition (20X8)	1,650
Less fair value of net assets at acquisition (W)	(5,100)
Goodwill at acquisition	1,550
Less impairment	0
Goodwill at the reporting date	**1,550**

(W) Net assets of IVY as at acquisition 31 January 20X8

	$000
Share capital	1,000
Retained earnings	3,650
Fair value adjustment – non-depreciable land	450
	5,100

5.2 C

Non-controlling interest as at 31 January 20X5

	$m
Fair value of non-controlling interest at acquisition (20X4)	3.3
Plus NCI % of S's post-acquisition movement in net assets (25% × 3.2 (W1))	0.8
NCI at 31 January 20X5	4.1

ANSWERS TO OBJECTIVE TEST QUESTIONS : SECTION 2

(W1) Net assets of VI

	At reporting date	At acquisition date	Post-acquisition
	$m	$m	$m
Share capital	2.0	2.0	–
Retained earnings	10.5	7.3	3.2
Fair value adjustment – non-depreciable land	0.9	0.9	
	13.4	10.2	3.2

5.3 A

Investment in associate (BO) as at 31 January 20X9

	$000
Cost of investment	8,000
Plus P% of associates' post-acquisition movement in net assets (30% × (1,250k – 2,200k))	(285)
Impairment	(500)
Investment in associate at 31 January 20X9	**7,215**

5.4 B

If SH's market share has been reduced by the new product on the market, yet SH's revenue has still increased in comparison to last year, this would suggest that the overall sporting technology market is in growth.

Option A is incorrect as it appears SH has reduced their operating costs. This is indicated by the gross profit margin reducing during the year yet the operating profit margin has increased. Increased marketing expenditure would be expected to reduce the operating margin during the year. It is possible that the marketing spend did increase but operating costs savings occurred elsewhere, however there is not enough information given to make that conclusion.

Option C cannot be concluded from the information given. An increase in payment terms from suppliers may have caused the increase in SH's payable days. However, the payables increase could also be caused by the lack of cash to pay suppliers. This is evident due to the use of an overdraft during the period. It cannot be concluded that an increase in supplier credit terms caused the increase.

Option D is not a valid conclusion. SH is using an overdraft which can be an indicator of some liquidity issues. There is no evidence to suggest that the overdraft usage is in breach of SH's authorised limits. As such, it cannot be concluded that SH is insolvent.

SUBJECT F2: ADVANCED FINANCIAL REPORTING

5.5 C

A lessor will need to determine whether a lease is a finance or operating lease. A finance lease is evidenced by the transfer of risk and rewards to the lessee. As the lease term is equal to the useful lifetime, this would suggest the lease is a finance lease, not an operating lease. Option A is incorrect.

The lessor, when accounting for finance leases, will derecognise the asset, record a lease receivable at the net investment in the lease and record a gain or loss on disposal.

The lease receivable will be initially calculated as the present value of future lease payments:

Cash flow	Discount factor (@10%)	Present value $
12,000	2.487	29,844

The initial entry is Dr Cash $5,000 Dr Lease receivable $29,844 Cr PPE 20,000 Cr Gain on disposal $14,844. Option C is correct.

The outstanding receivable is $29,844 as the deposit is paid in cash so is no longer outstanding. Option B considers the deposit to still be outstanding so is incorrect.

Interest income will increase the receivable by 10% per annum. The lease was entered into after 6 months of the year. Only 6 months of interest income would be recorded during 20X7 being $1,492 (10% × 29,844 × 6/12). Option D considered a full year of interest income.

5.6 B

Published financial statements should not contain material errors, as, for most companies, financial statements have been audited. Non-material errors will be contained within the financial statements but should not be of a magnitude that will impact the trends of ratio analysis. Errors are not a limitation of ratio analysis; they are a problem with the preparation of financial statements.

5.7 B

Basic EPS = $4,200,000/4,713,333 (W1) = 89.1c

(W1) Weighted average number of shares

Step 1 – Theoretical ex-rights price (TERP)

2 shares @ $2 =	$4
1 share @ $1.40 =	$1.40
3 shares	$5.40

TERP = $5.40/3 = $1.80

Step 2 – Rights issue bonus fraction

Cum rights price	2.00
Theoretical ex rights price	1.80

Step 3 – Weighted average number of shares

Date	Number	Fraction of year	Rights fraction	Weighted Average
1 January	3,360,000	3/12	2/1.8	933,333
1 April	5,040,000	9/12		3,780,000
				4,713,333

5.8 9.61%

Year	Cash flow	Discount factor at 5%	Present value	Discount factor at 10%	Present value
0	−98	1.000	**−98**	1.000	**−98**
1–3	5	2.723	**13.62**	2.487	**12.44**
3	112.5	0.864	**97.20**	0.751	**84.49**
			12.82		**−1.07**

YTM = 5% + [(10% − 5%) × 12.82/(12.82 + 1.07)] = 9.61%

5.9 D

Non-monetary assets are initially recorded at historic rate and require no further adjustment as at the reporting date. Option A is incorrect.

Foreign currency gains or loss arising from the translation of a foreign subsidiary within the group accounts are recorded within other comprehensive income. Option B is incorrect.

The functional currency is the currency used in an entity's primary economic environment. The presentation currency is the currency used to prepare the financial statements. Typically, they are one and the same but not exclusively so. For example, the functional currency of a foreign subsidiary may be different to the currency used to present the group financial statements (the group's presentation currency).

5.10 D

Human capital is affected by the staff of an entity. It will include staff's competencies and motivation to work within an organisation. High staff turnover indicates a dissatisfaction of staff to work for the company and will decrease human capital.

Section 3

REFERENCES

The Board (2021) *Conceptual Framework for Financial Reporting*. London: IFRS Foundation.

The Board (2021) *IAS 7 Statement of Cash Flows*. London: IFRS Foundation.

The Board (2021) *IAS 12 Income Taxes*. London: IFRS Foundation.

The Board (2021) *IAS 21 The Effects of Changes in Foreign Exchange Rates*. London: IFRS Foundation.

The Board (2021) *IAS 24 Related Party Disclosures*. London: IFRS Foundation.

The Board (2021) *IAS 27 Separate Financial Statements*. London: IFRS Foundation.

The Board (2021) *IAS 28 Investments in Associates and Joint Ventures*. London: IFRS Foundation.

The Board (2021) *IAS 32 Financial Instruments: Presentation*. London: IFRS Foundation.

The Board (2021) *IAS 33 Earnings per Share*. London: IFRS Foundation.

The Board (2021) *IAS 37 Provisions, Contingent Liabilities and Contingent Assets*. London: IFRS Foundation.

The Board (2021) *IAS 38 Intangible Assets*. London: IFRS Foundation.

The Board (2021) *IFRS 3 Business Combinations*. London: IFRS Foundation.

The Board (2021) *IFRS 7 Financial Instruments: Disclosure*. London: IFRS Foundation.

The Board (2021) *IFRS 9 Financial Instruments*. London: IFRS Foundation.

The Board (2021) *IFRS 10 Consolidated Financial Statements*. London: IFRS Foundation.

The Board (2021) *IFRS 11 Joint Arrangements*. London: IFRS Foundation.

The Board (2021) *IFRS 12 Disclosure of Interests in Other Entities*. London: IFRS Foundation.

The Board (2021) *IFRS 13 Fair Value Measurement*. London: IFRS Foundation.

The Board (2021) *IFRS 15 Revenue from contracts with customers*. London: IFRS Foundation.

The Board (2021) *IFRS 16 Leases*. London: IFRS Foundation.